Full Stack Web Development with Raspberry Pi 3

Build complex web applications with a portable computer

Soham Kamani

BIRMINGHAM - MUMBAI

Full Stack Web Development with Raspberry Pi 3

First published: August 2017

Production reference: 1020817

Published by Packt Publishing Ltd.
Livery Place
35 Livery Street
Birmingham
B3 2PB, UK.

ISBN 978-1-78829-589-5

www.packtpub.com

Credits

Author
Soham Kamani

Copy Editor
Stuti Srivastava

Reviewers
Avron Bernard Olshewsky
Krishnaraj Varma

Project Coordinator
Virginia Dias

Commissioning Editor
Vijin Boricha

Proofreader
Safis Editing

Acquisition Editor
Meeta Rajani

Indexer
Aishwarya Gangawane

Content Development Editor
Sweeny Dias

Graphics
Kirk D'Penha

Technical Editor
Prashant Chaudhari

Production Coordinator
Aparna Bhagat

About the Author

Soham Kamani is a full-stack developer who has extensive experience in the JavaScript ecosystem. He works as a consultant, developing end-to-end web-based solutions for clients around the world. He is an open source enthusiast and an avid blogger. He has worked on many frameworks and technologies such as React, Angular, Node, Express, Sails, SQLite, Postgres, and MySQL, and he has worked on many projects in the IoT space using Arduino and Raspberry Pi systems.

About the Reviewers

Avron Bernard Olshewsky is an entrepreneurial technologist with a background in server-side telecommunication software engineering. Since 2006, he has worked as a founder, advisor, and consultant for technology start-up companies and small businesses. He has over 20 years of commercial software engineering experience, developing and leading innovative software solutions. In addition to advising start-ups on technology viability, architecture, specification, the resources required, funding, and roadmap, he has also been involved with long-established companies such as T-Mobile, Motorola, and IBM in various engineering capacities.

Krishnaraj Varma is a software professional and a tech enthusiast from Kerala, India. Primarily a software architect and a programmer, he started programming in the 90s in DBMS such as dBase and Clipper. After that, he started coding in C and C++ and continues to do so because of his vast interest in these languages. His areas of expertise are Internet of Things, Big Data, real-time streaming pipelines.

Apart from coding and technology, he is interested in nature, movies, and music.

www.PacktPub.com

For support files and downloads related to your book, please visit www.PacktPub.com.

Did you know that Packt offers eBook versions of every book published, with PDF and ePub files available? You can upgrade to the eBook version at www.PacktPub.com, and as a print book customer, you are entitled to a discount on the eBook copy. Get in touch with us at service@packtpub.com for more details.

At www.PacktPub.com, you can also read a collection of free technical articles, sign up for a range of free newsletters and receive exclusive discounts and offers on Packt books and eBooks.

https://www.packtpub.com/mapt

Get the most in-demand software skills with Mapt. Mapt gives you full access to all Packt books and video courses, as well as industry-leading tools to help you plan your personal development and advance your career.

Why subscribe?

- Fully searchable across every book published by Packt
- Copy and paste, print, and bookmark content
- On demand and accessible via a web browser

Customer Feedback

Thanks for purchasing this Packt book. At Packt, quality is at the heart of our editorial process. To help us improve, please leave us an honest review on this book's Amazon page at https://www.amazon.com/dp/1788295897.

If you'd like to join our team of regular reviewers, you can e-mail us at customerreviews@packtpub.com. We award our regular reviewers with free eBooks and videos in exchange for their valuable feedback. Help us be relentless in improving our products!

Table of Contents

Preface

Just a few decades back, the average computer was the size of an entire city block and could barely store 5 MB of data. Today, this amount of data is consumed by an average image upload, and the dimensions of the modern computer have reached a stage where we can hold one on the palm of our hands. Alongside the reduction in size, computers have also undergone a tremendous reduction in cost. Raspberry Pi is the flag bearer of portable and affordable computing, barely costing $30 and being small enough to be held in your hand.

The introduction of Raspberry Pi has opened the doors for applications that would not have been feasible otherwise, and that is precisely what you will learn from this book.

In the chapters to follow, you will learn how Raspberry Pi can be utilized to its full potential and act as a sensor interface, a web server, and a database and host all the components of a fully functioning web application. You will also learn how to utilize cloud-based APIs and data storage and combine this with the existing components developed on Raspberry Pi to make an application that can accessed by anyone with an internet connection.

What this book covers

Chapter 1, *Getting Started on the Raspberry Pi* , takes a brief look at Raspberry Pi, its OS, and how to get started using it

Chapter 2, *Getting Up-and-Running with Web Development on the Raspberry Pi*, covers a high-level overview of the project that we will build and the different components of its technology stack.

Chapter 3, *Running a Node Server on the Pi*, helps you get started with Node.js, its installation on the Pi, and how to get up and running with Node.js by running a web server on the Pi.

Chapter 4, *Extracting Information from the GPIO Pins*, introduces you to the DHT22 sensor and demonstrates how to get information about the temperature and humidity recorded from the sensor.

Chapter 5, *Retrieving Sensor Readings from the Server*, goes through how to make the sensor readings available to the node server that was made earlier. By the end of this chapter, you will know how to make sensor readings available through a REST API.

Chapter 6, *Creating a Web Page to Display Sensor Data*, gets you started with your UI development journey by developing a webpage that will make use of the API created in the previous chapter to display the data received from the sensor in a user-friendly webpage.

Chapter 7, *Enhancing Our UI - Using Interactive Charts*, covers how to make an even richer user interface through the use of charts. This will be achieved through the use of open source chart libraries

Chapter 8, *SQLite - The Fast and Portable Database*, covers the basic concepts of the SQLite database and teaches you how to install and run it on your Pi.

Chapter 9, *Integrating SQLite into Our Application*, explains how to upgrade our existing application built in the previous chapters by persisting our data.

Chapter 10, *Making Our Application Real Time with Web Sockets*, discusses how all this time, the only way for our HTML5 frontend to get data from the server was through polling and making requests at regular intervals. Web sockets allow us to establish a connection only once, after which the server can actually push data to the browser.

Chapter 11, *Deploying Our Application to Firebase*, reiterates that our entire application is currently hosted on the Raspberry Pi. This works, but is not very scalable. This chapter will go through how to host our UI and database on Google's Firebase cloud architecture.

Chapter 12, *Using Firebase APIs to Update Our Application*, covers how to update the database by calling Firebase's cloud APIs from Raspberry Pi so that the cloud hosted application can get a continuous feed of the readings on the Pi.

What you need for this book

The reader should have some basic knowledge and programming experience (in any programming language). An awareness of the basic concepts regarding HTML and JavaScript would be a plus point, but is not required, and of will be covered in brief in this book. The reader is also expected to have a base level understanding of electronic hardware (how to connect pins and wires).

To execute all the examples given in this book, you will need the following:

- A Raspberry Pi board, which will be the device where all the code is executed
- Monitor, keyboard, and mouse to interact with the Raspbian OS
- Memory card for the Raspberry Pi
- Personal computer (optional), although this book is designed such that the entire application can be built and executed on the Pi, having a computer handy can help a lot.

Who this book is for

This book is aimed at hobbyist, enthusiasts, and developers eager to develop embedded device-powered web applications. Prior programming experience with JavaScript, HTML5, and Node.js will be beneficial.

Conventions

In this book, you will find a number of text styles that distinguish between different kinds of information. Here are some examples of these styles and an explanation of their meaning. Code words in text, database table names, folder names, filenames, file extensions, pathnames, dummy URLs, user input, and Twitter handles are shown as follows: "Most of these files have no meaning to us except the INSTRUCTIONS-README.txt file."

A block of code is set as follows:

```
app.get('/temperature', function(req, res) {
res.send('24 °C');
});
```

Any command-line input or output is written as follows:

```
firebase --version
```

New terms and **important words** are shown in bold. Words that you see on the screen, for example, in menus or dialog boxes, appear in the text like this: "In the Firebase console, go to the **SERVICE ACCOUNTS** section of your application settings."

Warnings or important notes appear like this.

 Tips and tricks appear like this.

Reader feedback

Feedback from our readers is always welcome. Let us know what you think about this book-what you liked or disliked. Reader feedback is important for us as it helps us develop titles that you will really get the most out of. To send us general feedback, simply e-mail feedback@packtpub.com, and mention the book's title in the subject of your message. If there is a topic that you have expertise in and you are interested in either writing or contributing to a book, see our author guide at www.packtpub.com/authors.

Customer support

Now that you are the proud owner of a Packt book, we have a number of things to help you to get the most from your purchase.

Downloading the example code

You can download the example code files for this book from your account at http://www.packtpub.com. If you purchased this book elsewhere, you can visit http://www.packtpub.com/supportand register to have the files e-mailed directly to you. You can download the code files by following these steps:

1. Log in or register to our website using your e-mail address and password.
2. Hover the mouse pointer on the **SUPPORT** tab at the top.
3. Click on **Code Downloads & Errata**.
4. Enter the name of the book in the **Search** box.
5. Select the book for which you're looking to download the code files.
6. Choose from the drop-down menu where you purchased this book from.
7. Click on **Code Download**.

Once the file is downloaded, please make sure that you unzip or extract the folder using the latest version of:

- WinRAR / 7-Zip for Windows
- Zipeg / iZip / UnRarX for Mac
- 7-Zip / PeaZip for Linux

The code bundle for the book is also hosted on GitHub at `https://github.com/PacktPubl ishing/Full-Stack-Web-Development-with-Raspberry-Pi-3/`. We also have other code bundles from our rich catalog of books and videos available at `https://git hub.com/PacktPublishing/`. Check them out!

Downloading the color images of this book

We also provide you with a PDF file that has color images of the screenshots/diagrams used in this book. The color images will help you better understand the changes in the output. You can download this file from `https://www.packtpub.com/sites/default/files/down loads/FullStackWebDevelopmentwithRaspberryPi3_ColorImages.pdf`.

Errata

Although we have taken every care to ensure the accuracy of our content, mistakes do happen. If you find a mistake in one of our books-maybe a mistake in the text or the code-we would be grateful if you could report this to us. By doing so, you can save other readers from frustration and help us improve subsequent versions of this book. If you find any errata, please report them by visiting `http://www.packtpub.com/submit-errata`, selecting your book, clicking on the **Errata Submission Form** link, and entering the details of your errata. Once your errata are verified, your submission will be accepted and the errata will be uploaded to our website or added to any list of existing errata under the Errata section of that title. To view the previously submitted errata, go to `https://www.packtpub.com/book s/content/support` and enter the name of the book in the search field. The required information will appear under the **Errata** section.

Piracy

Piracy of copyrighted material on the Internet is an ongoing problem across all media. At Packt, we take the protection of our copyright and licenses very seriously. If you come across any illegal copies of our works in any form on the Internet, please provide us with the location address or website name immediately so that we can pursue a remedy. Please contact us at copyright@packtpub.com with a link to the suspected pirated material. We appreciate your help in protecting our authors and our ability to bring you valuable content.

Questions

If you have a problem with any aspect of this book, you can contact us at questions@packtpub.com, and we will do our best to address the problem.

1
Getting Started on the Raspberry Pi

The Raspberry Pi has become hugely popular as a portable computer, and for good reason. When it comes to what you can do with this tiny piece of technology, the sky's the limit. Back in the day, computers used to be the size of entire neighborhood blocks, and only large corporations doing expensive research could afford them. After that, we went on to embrace personal computers, which were still a bit expensive, but, for the most part, could be bought by the common man. This brings us to where we are today, where we can buy a fully functioning Linux computer, which is as big as a credit card, for under $30. It is truly a huge leap in making computers available to anyone and everyone.

The marvel of the Raspberry Pi, however, doesn't end here. Its extreme portability means we can now do things that were not previously possible with traditional desktop computers. The GPIO pins give us easy access to interface with external devices. This allows the Pi to act as a bridge between embedded electronics and sensors and the power that Linux gives us. In essence, we can run any code in our favorite programming language (which can run on Linux) and interface it directly to outside hardware quickly and easily. Once we couple this with the wireless networking capabilities introduced in the Raspberry Pi 3, we gain the ability to make applications that would not have been feasible to make before this device existed.

Web development and portable computing have come a long way. A few years ago, we couldn't dream of making a rich, interactive, and performant application that runs on the browser. Today, not only can we do that, but we can also do it all in the palm of our hands (quite literally). When we think of developing an application that uses databases, application servers, sockets, and cloud APIs, the picture that normally comes to mind is that of many server racks sitting in a huge room. In this book, however, we are going to implement all of that using only the Raspberry Pi.

In this chapter, we will go through the concept of the Internet of Things and discuss how web development on the Raspberry Pi can help us get there. Following this, you will also learn how to set up your Raspberry Pi and access it from our computer.

We will cover the following topics:

- The **Internet of Things (IoT)**
- Our application
- Setting up the Raspberry Pi
- Remote access

The Internet of Things

The web has, until today, been a network of computers exchanging data. The limitation of this was that it was a closed loop. People could send and receive data from other people via their computers but rarely much else.

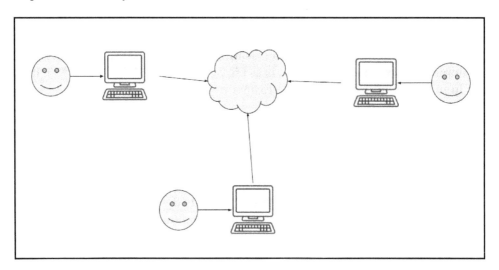

The IoT, in contrast, is a network of devices or sensors that connect the outside world to the internet. Superficially, nothing is different: the internet is still a network of computers. What has changed is that now, these computers are collecting and uploading data from things instead of people. This now allows anyone who is connected to obtain information that is not collected by a human.

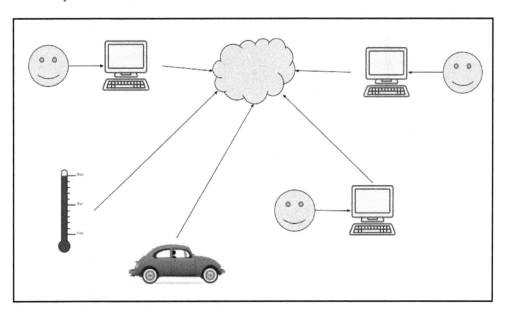

The IoT as a concept has been around for a long time, but it is only now that almost anyone can connect a sensor or device to the cloud, and the IoT revolution was hugely enabled by the advent of portable computing, which was led by the Raspberry Pi.

A brief look at our application

Throughout this book, we are going to go through different components and aspects of web development and embedded systems. These are all going to be held together by our central goal of making an entire web application capable of sensing and displaying the surrounding temperature and humidity.

In order to make a properly functioning system, we have to first build the individual parts. More difficult still is making sure all the parts work well together. Keeping this in mind, let's take a look at the different components of our technology stack and the problems that each of them solves:

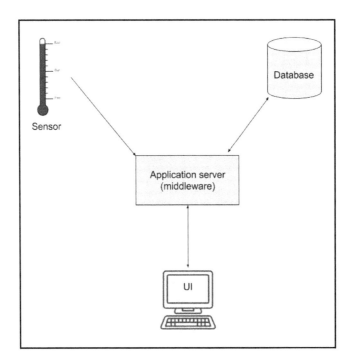

The sensor interface - perception

The sensor is what connects our otherwise isolated application to the outside world. The sensor will be connected to the GPIO pins of the Raspberry Pi. We can interface with the sensor through various different native libraries, which we will be looking into in the later chapters.

This is the starting point of our data. It is where all the data that is used by our application is created. If you think about it, every other component of our technology stack exists only to manage, manipulate, and display the data collected from the sensor.

The database - persistence

Data is the name we give to raw information, which is information that we cannot easily aggregate or understand. Without a way to store and meaningfully process and retrieve this data, it will always remain *data* and never *information*, which is what we actually want.

If we just hook up a sensor and display whatever data it reads, we are missing out on a lot of additional information. Let's take the example of temperature: what if we wanted to find out *how* the temperature was changing over time? What if we wanted to find the maximum and minimum temperatures for a particular day, or a particular week, or even within a custom duration of time? What if we wanted to see temperature variation across locations? There is no way we could do any of this with only the sensor. We also need some sort of persistence and structure to our data, and this is exactly what the database provides for us.

If we structure our data correctly, getting the answers to these questions is just a matter of a simple database query.

The user interface - presentation

The user interface is the layer that connects our application to the end user. One of the most challenging aspects of software development is making information meaningful and understandable to regular users of our application.

The UI layer serves exactly this purpose: it takes relevant information and shows it in such a way that it is easily understandable to humans. How do we achieve such a level of understandability with such a large amount of data? We use visual aids, such as colors, charts, and diagrams (just like how the diagrams in this book make the information easier to understand).

An important thing for any developer to understand is that your end user actually doesn't care about any of the backend stuff. The only thing that matters to them is a good experience. Of course, all the other components serve to make the users experience better, but it's really the user facing interface that leaves the first impression, and that's why it's so important to do it well.

The application server - middleware

This layer consists of the actual server-side code we are going to write in order to get the application running. It is also called **middleware**. In addition to being in the exact center of the architecture diagram, this layer also acts as the controller and middle-man for the other layers.

The HTML pages that form the UI are served through this layer. All the database queries that we were talking about earlier are made here. The code that runs in this layer is responsible for retrieving the sensor readings from our external pins and storing the data in our database. As you will see in later chapters, the middleware can also be further broken down into individual components, each with its own function.

Setting up our Raspberry Pi

So far, we've been reading a lot of theory. Now let's actually get our Raspberry Pi working. Before we get started, here is a list of things you need at the bare minimum to get your Pi up-and-running:

- The Raspberry Pi (duh)
- An SD card (8 GB or higher)
- A micro USB power source (many phone chargers are of this type so you might have one already)
- A keyboard and mouse
- Any screen or display with an HDMI port and cable
- A laptop (optional)

Have everything? Awesome! Let's move on...

There are lots of operating systems and lots of ways to install them on the Pi. However, the easiest way by far is to use the official NOOBS installer. **NOOBS**, which stands for **New Out Of Box Software**, is the officially recommended way to install a fresh OS on the Pi for newcomers, and it's terribly easy.

Download the NOOBS archive from official website (`https://www.raspberrypi.org/down loads/noobs/`). Once the archive is downloaded, unzip it into a new folder anywhere on your computer.

If you are using NOOBS v2.3.0, the directory structure, once you unzip the archive, should look like this:

```
BUILD-DATA
INSTRUCTIONS-README.txt
RECOVERY_FILES_DO_NOT_EDIT
bcm2708-rpi-0-w.dtb
bcm2708-rpi-b-plus.dtb
bcm2708-rpi-b.dtb
bcm2708-rpi-cm.dtb
bcm2709-rpi-2-b.dtb
bcm2710-rpi-3-b.dtb
bcm2710-rpi-cm3.dtb
bootcode.bin
defaults
os
overlays
recovery.cmdline
recovery.elf
recovery.img
recovery.rfs
recovery7.img
riscos-boot.bin
```

Most of these files have no meaning to us except the `INSTRUCTIONS-README.txt` file. Open this file in any text editor (such as Notepad), and you will find instructions on how to format your SD card.

After formatting your SD card, transfer all these files and folders to the root directory of the SD card. As described in the instructions, all files and folders should be copied in such a way that the `INSTRUCTIONS-README.txt` file is at the root.

Once your SD card is ready and loaded, connect everything to your Pi:

1. Insert the SD card into the slot.
2. Using the **HDMI** cable, connect the HDMI port of the Pi with the external display.
3. Connect the keyboard and mouse to the USB ports of the Pi
4. Connect the power cable to the **Micro USB** port of the Pi

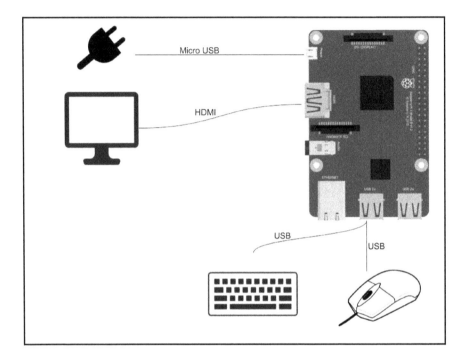

Once all the connections are made, switch on the power supply to your Pi. You should now see the monitor light up. After a few boot screens, you should see a friendly little GUI that will lead you to this:

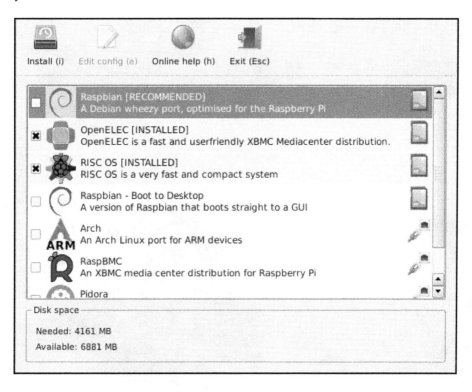

It's here that you can select the OS you want in order to install to your Pi. For this book, we will be working with Raspbian.

Raspbian is a port of the Debian Linux OS, that has been optimized for the Pi. It is currently the most popular OS that runs on the Pi. Follow the installation wizard, and you should be done with the installation in a few minutes.

Once your installation is done, your Pi will boot into the OS, and you should now see a complete desktop on your monitor screen, something that looks like this:

Congratulations! You have successfully set up your Raspberry Pi computer. Amazingly, there are a lot of things you can do like you're using a regular desktop computer. The Raspberry Pi, along with the Raspbian OS, comes with a variety of programs, such as a text editor, a file explorer, and even an HTML5 web browser!

Remote access

The setup we have here is perfectly sufficient for moving on with the rest of the chapters. You now have a fully functioning Raspberry Pi running and now have the capability to run a fully functioning web application on it.

Yet, for those who prefer programming on their laptop (and most people do), it would make sense to be able to remotely access and program on the Raspberry Pi using our computer of choice.

Fortunately for us, it's really easy to do this. Sometimes, I even prefer remotely programming my Pi from my laptop because it's much easier and more convenient to do that.

To access our Pi, we are going to use SSH (secure shell) to access its shell from any computer on the network:

1. First things first, make sure your Pi is connected to the same network as your computer. If you are using a wired router, connect the Pi through it using a **LAN cable**:

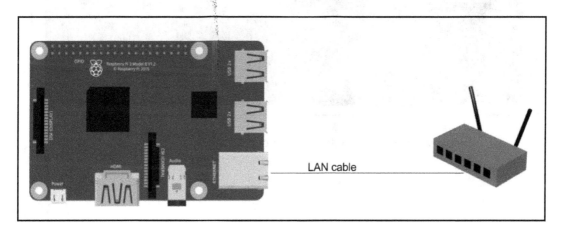

LAN cable

A better option, though, is to connect the Pi wirelessly through WLAN.

If you already have a wireless network running, connect your Pi to the network by clicking on the wireless network icon on the desktop:

Select your wireless network and connect to it.

2. The next step is to find the private IP address of your Pi. Open the Terminal application by clicking on the icon, as shown in the following screenshot:

Execute the `ifconfig` command in the Terminal window. The `ifconfig` command, if executed with no other arguments, will display the status of all network interfaces on the device. You should get an output that looks like this:

```
eth0      Link encap:Ethernet  HWaddr b8:27:eb:f6:fc:89
          inet6 addr: fe80::734f:7460:dcaf:cc40/64 Scope:Link
          UP BROADCAST MULTICAST  MTU:1500  Metric:1
          RX packets:0 errors:0 dropped:0 overruns:0 frame:0
          TX packets:0 errors:0 dropped:0 overruns:0 carrier:0
          collisions:0 txqueuelen:1000
          RX bytes:0 (0.0 B)  TX bytes:0 (0.0 B)

lo        Link encap:Local Loopback
          inet addr:127.0.0.1  Mask:255.0.0.0
          inet6 addr: ::1/128 Scope:Host
          UP LOOPBACK RUNNING  MTU:65536  Metric:1
          RX packets:209 errors:0 dropped:0 overruns:0 frame:0
          TX packets:209 errors:0 dropped:0 overruns:0 carrier:0
          collisions:0 txqueuelen:1
          RX bytes:17180 (16.7 KiB)  TX bytes:17180 (16.7 KiB)

wlan0     Link encap:Ethernet  HWaddr b8:27:eb:a3:a9:dc
          inet addr:192.168.0.10  Bcast:192.168.0.255  Mask:255.255.255.0
          inet6 addr: fe80::7610:934f:49b8:5252/64 Scope:Link
          UP BROADCAST RUNNING MULTICAST  MTU:1500  Metric:1
          RX packets:18681 errors:0 dropped:14902 overruns:0 frame:0
          TX packets:4620 errors:0 dropped:0 overruns:0 carrier:0
          collisions:0 txqueuelen:1000
          RX bytes:3576248 (3.4 MiB)  TX bytes:4214622 (4.0 MiB)
```

Your private IP address can be found by looking at the `inet addr` field (as highlighted in the preceding figure). Depending on the interface you are connected to, this address can appear either under `wlan0` (if you are connected using Wi-Fi) or `eth0` (if you connect with a LAN cable). My IP address, in this case, is `192.168.0.10`.

3. We need to now enable the SSH server on our Pi. This is the service that allows us to access our Pi's command line remotely. To do this, open the system configuration by running the following command:

3. `sudo raspi-config`

You should see a GUI-like configuration screen, as follows:

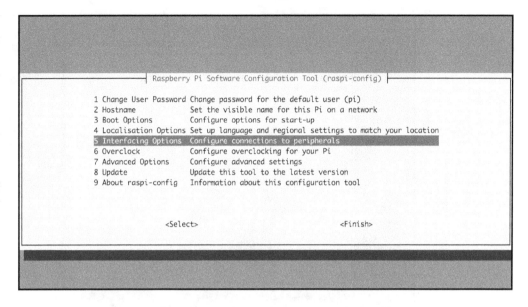

Go to the **Interfacing Options** section, and then go to **P2 SSH**.

You will then need to give a confirmation to start the SSH server.

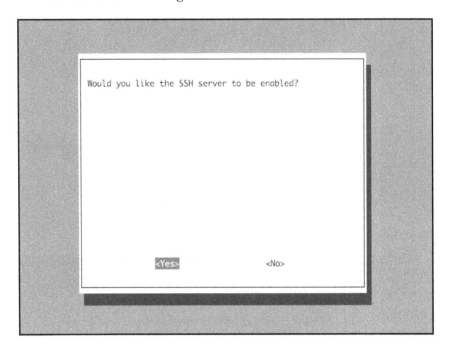

4. All that's left is to finally connect to the Raspberry Pi using our laptops or desktops.

If you are working on a Windows machine, you will need to download and install PuTTY (h ttp://www.putty.org/), which is a free SSH client for Windows. Enter the IP address of the Raspberry Pi, which we obtained in the previous step, with the port as 22 (the default SSH port).

If you are using a Unix system (Mac or Linux), you can ssh into the Pi by entering the following command:
```
ssh pi@192.168.0.10
```

 Remember to replace 192.168.0.10 with your own Pi's IP address.

In both cases, you will be asked for a password. The default username for the Raspbian OS after installation is `pi`, with the default password being `raspberry`. If you are able to establish an SSH session with the Pi, you should see its command prompt:

You can now remotely access your Raspberry Pi device from any computer on the network. Awesome!

What's even more awesome is that there is no need to connect any peripheral device to the Pi anymore. That means no mouse, no keyboard, and no monitor required! All you need is the power supply, and with SSH, you're good to go!

As I stated earlier, you need not go through the hassle of remotely accessing the Pi from your own computer. The Pi is a perfectly good standalone computer on its own. Many of your favorite text editors can also be run on the Pi, which means that you can write and execute code on the same Raspberry Pi device.

Summary

We are just warming up! In this chapter, we got a brief introduction to the concept of the Internet of Things. We then went on to look at an overview of what we were going to build throughout the rest of this book and saw how the Raspberry Pi can help us get there. The next section showed us how to get up and running with our Pi by installing and running the Raspbian OS.

Finally, you learned how to make life easier by being able to access the Pi remotely through our desktop or laptop.

This chapter essentially forms the base for us moving forward. It is important to make sure that you get the installation right, as we are going to rely solely on the Raspberry Pi's environment for the execution of our code. Our laptop is simply going to assist us in writing the code.

In the next chapter, we will dive deep into the web development stack and look at how each layer plays its role and how we can build them it forward.

2
Getting Up-and-Running with Web Development on the Raspberry Pi

The web is an amazing place. It's open, it's free, and almost all the information available to human kind is available any time, any place, and right at our fingertips. It is amazing that we live in an age when the web is just starting to show its colors and full potential. However, if you look at it from another point of view, all the internet really is is just a bunch of computers connected together with wires or, sometimes, wirelessly. It is this illusion that gives us the impression that the internet is actually something bigger, when in fact it's just a large network of computers.

After you are done with this book, you will be adding one more computer to this network, thus doing your own bit to make the internet a better place. To understand how the internet works, we have to first understand the role of each computer or component of the network. To do this, consider the following questions:

- Where does all the information on the internet come from?
- Where is it stored?
- How is it given to us?
- How do we interact with it?

By the end of this chapter, you should be able to answer these questions and also see how the Raspberry Pi can implement all these aspects of the web.
Specifically, we will cover the following topics:

- The overall architecture of a full-stack web application
- Different layers of web development
- Communication between the different layers of the stack
- How the Raspberry Pi will incorporate these layers and its role as a client and a server.

The network

A single computer on its own can achieve a lot, but its capability becomes exponentially larger when it can communicate with other computers. This communication occurs among computers that belong to the same network.

A computer can be a part of a network through various means: such as an Ethernet cable or through Wi-Fi. In the previous chapter, we observed the output of the `ifconfig` command, which showed us the different interfaces through which our device could possibly be connected.

Now that we know a network can have multiple computers, the next question that arises is about how each computer is identified on the network. This is what each device's IP address (or IPv4 address, to be more precise) is used for. It specifies the location and acts as an identifier for each device connected to a network.

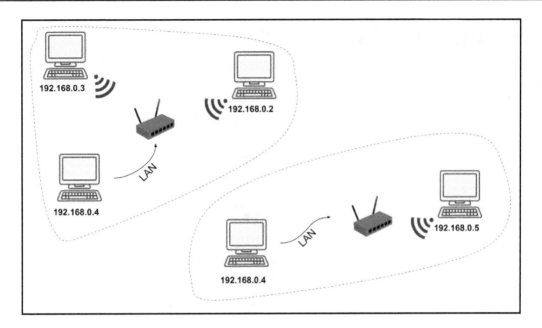

The dotted boundary in the figure represents a single network. For each individual network, every device must have a unique IP address. This IP address is only unique for a single network. If you notice, there are two devices that have the IP address of 192.168.0.4, which is fine since they are on different networks.

 Each IP address is specific only to a single network, and each device can only have one IP address.

Our Raspberry Pi is nothing special. In the previous chapter, we found the Pi's IP address for the network that it was connected to.

Although each device has its own IP address, there will still be many services running on it. For example, we can have a web server and database running on our Pi at the same time, and both services must be communicated with independently. This is what **ports** are for.

Each port on a single device refers to one single service running on that device. As a principle, every program that needs to communicate with the outside world requires a port. Each device has port numbers ranging from 0 to 65535. Ports ranging from 0 till 1024 are reserved, and any port numbers after that can be used for our applications. Since we will be running most of our services on our Pi device itself, we will use a different port for each of them.

The web development stack

A development stack is actually a very loosely defined term, which actually refers to the list of technologies and frameworks that you need in order to get an application up-and-running. It's called a **stack** because each layer is more and more abstracted from the user. Consider the example of the popular **MEAN** stack (**MongoDB**, **Express**, **AngularJS**, **Node.js**). If we were to actually make a physical stack out of these, it would look like this:

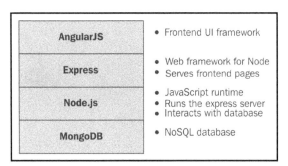

AngularJS is served by the **Express** server, which is run by the **Node.js** JavaScript runtime, which in turn is able to interact with the **MongoDB** database.

What's important to note is that as we move down the stack, each layer gets more and more inaccessible to the user of our application:

- The user has full and uninhibited access to the frontend Angular code.
- There is limited interaction with the **Express** server, normally through the use of HTTP requests that the server responds to.
- There is no direct interaction between the user and the database or the node runtime. If you ever build an application where your users have direct access to your database, there are serious security concerns.

Let's take the example of the very application we are going to build with this book so that we can have some context to understand the web development stack better.

As with any generic stack, it's conventional to look at it from a top-down approach, that is, looking at each layer, starting from the one on top, and slowly uncovering the layers at the bottom. Let's follow this approach by analyzing what we require from the very first layer of our stack and working our way down to solve the challenges we face.

The UI - the user's first encounter

The **user interface** (**UI**) is, quite literally, the part that acts as the interface between our user and our application. It is the only direct point of contact that the user will have with our app (unless they decide to get creative).

Here is a brief summary of what we want our user interface to do:

- Be accessible from a wide variety of devices anywhere in the World (as much as possible)
- Show the user the current temperature and humidity reading
- Show the history of the temperature and humidity for the last week
- Have the ability to view temperature and humidity details for any point in time in the past
- Update the temperature shown to the user as soon as a new reading is obtained

Satisfying the first requirement means that we have to choose a platform to develop, which requires the least effort to access and install. The obvious choice for this is HTML5:

- HTML5 runs on almost any device you can think of: on mobile and tablet browsers, on the desktop, and even on the Raspberry Pi
- It does not require any installation to run our application on a mobile device, unlike the native apps on the app store

Besides being omnipresent, developing on HTML5 and the web has other benefits:

- There is no need to develop for each operating system. You develop once, and it runs everywhere.
- There are tools available to port any app you develop for the web to native mobile applications (such as **Cordova**: `https://cordova.apache.org/`) and even desktop applications (such as the **Electron** framework: `https://electron.atom.io/`)

The second point requires that we have some sort of access to the temperature reading. In this case, we will leave it to the server (API layer) to provide us with this information (which we will cover in a bit).

The third and fourth point tell us to show a certain amount of historical data, with the option given to the user of changing the time period of the data shown. This means we cannot simply show temperature and humidity readings as and when they come. We have to record them as well. Again, this is not the job of the UI, and we will leave this task for the layers further down the stack. What we should do in this layer is display this information intuitively.

The last point has to do with introducing a real-time component. This can be harder than it seems, as we will see in the next section.

The server - the brains of the application

The server or middleware layer is the part of your tech stack that interacts with and controls all the other parts.

All of the frontend HTML5 code runs only on the client's machine. This means that if someone views your website on their phone, the code that the frontend of the website is built in is run *on* their phone. In contrast, the server-side code is executed on the serving machine. In our case, this will be the Raspberry Pi. In this way, we have two machines involved so far - the client and the server.

Client-server communication

The client and the server communicate many times and in different ways.

The first instance of communication occurs when the code that executes on the client machine has to be sent. We mentioned earlier that one of the advantages of using the web as opposed to native apps is that we would not have to install them all the time. As it turns out, this comes with some trade-offs as well, because every time we visit a website, we have to download all of its layout and code. Most commonly, this is in the form of HTML (for layout), CSS (for style), and JavaScript (for functionality).

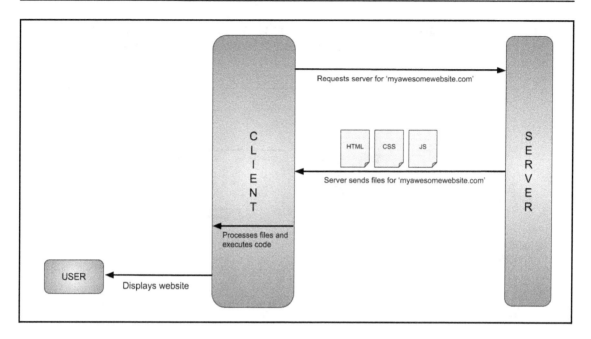

The preceding figure shows the simplest models of client-server communication on the web, where the client executes and displays what the server sends it.

One of the steps in the previous figure entails processing and executing the code sent by the server. In richer and more complex applications, the execution of code itself can lead to more requests being made to the server. In our case, we want to display a constantly changing temperature and humidity to the user. It would be quite a poor experience for the user if they had to refresh and download the files all over again just to see the new readings.

One approach we can take to solving this problem is making repeated requests to the server at fixed time intervals in order to get new values. Once we get this information, we can update the UI.

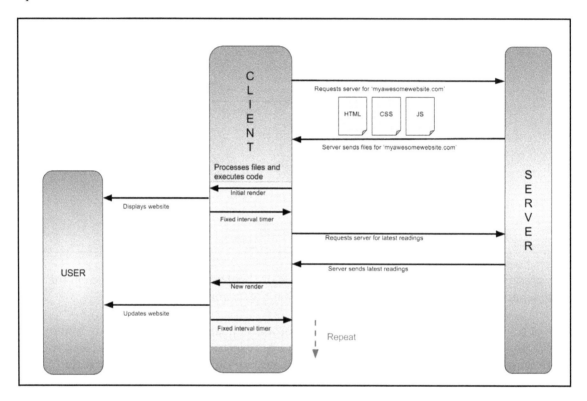

These HTTP requests that are made by the web page itself are called **AJAX** requests (**Asynchronous JavaScript** and **XML**). AJAX requests are different from traditional HTTP requests in that they do not request and load the entire web page all over again. Instead, they only request for the information that is needed. In our case, this is the current information about the temperature and humidity.

One limitation with this process is that it is the browser that has to make a request to the server each time it wants new data. This process of polling is not always efficient because of the following reasons:

- The browser has to constantly request for the new temperature readings at fixed intervals regardless of whether they have actually changed

- Even when the readings have changed, it only update on the frontend as and when the browser polls for new readings again

Both of these problems are solved by making use of a more advanced mode of communication, called web sockets. The main cause of these issues is that the server cannot notify the browser. It can only provide information when the browser requests for it. This restriction is mainly there for security reasons, but it's still a pain to handle when you want true real-time updates. Web sockets provide a solution to this problem by allowing the server to push information to the browser. This is done after the browser and server both establish a socket connection with each other. Instead of the request-response model, the browser and server both create a channel between each other, after which information can be sent across the channel, either from the browser to the server or vice-versa.

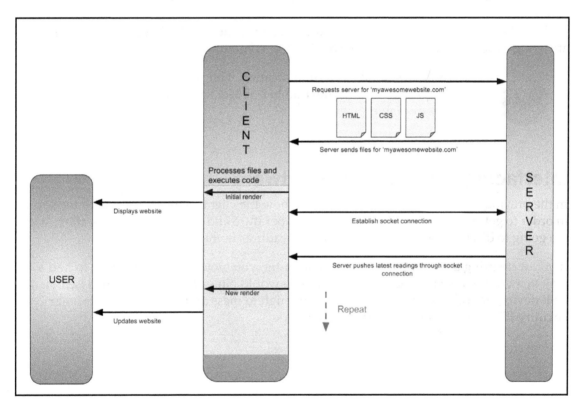

Now we have solved both of the limitations we were facing earlier. The trade-off with using web sockets, however, is that they take more resources to manage on the server side, so while it's great to use sockets if you only have a few users, you might want to look at how your application would scale as your user-base grows. Additionally, web sockets are not supported on older and legacy browsers, so only use them if you are sure your user-base has access to newer versions of browsers.

So far, we have discussed three methods of client-server communication:

- Standard HTTP requests
- AJAX requests
- Web sockets

Each method comes with its own pros and cons, and while developing our application, we are going to be making use of all three methods of communication.

 There is no best mode of communication. You should make a choice based on the application needs, the number of users expected, and the system resources available.

Interfacing with external hardware

In the previous section, we were talking about how the client communicates with the server in order to get the latest readings about the temperature and humidity. In this section, we are going to discuss how the server gets these readings in the first place.

If you were using a regular old laptop or computer, you would be hard pressed to find a way to measure the world outside directly. You would either need to get a pre-assembled USB device, or you would have to be smart enough to mess around with the computer circuitry. Either way, none of these are pragmatic.

The Raspberry Pi, however, excels in this area. One of its key features is its **GPIO pins**:

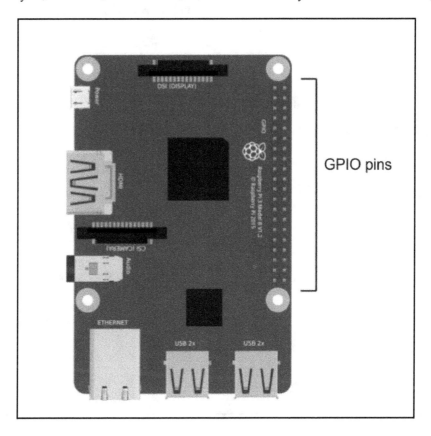

These pins allow us to directly connect any sensor and read its output. This is done through native system calls, which are exposed through convenient command-line utilities (which we will be discussing in detail in the later chapters). Our server can make these calls, read their output, and pass on the result to the client-side application. In this way, the server layer acts as a middleman between the sensor and client-side interfaces (hence the name middleware)

It is possible that the language we write our server in could be different from the language that is used to interface with some sensors. For example, the DTH11 temperature and humidity sensors have good support in Python libraries, but not much else. In this situation, in order to make communication between the server program and the sensor program easier, we can use two different methods.

The first method involves communication through subprocesses. The server, which is a process itself, spawns the sensor process as its own child process. It gives input to this child process and receives any of the output.

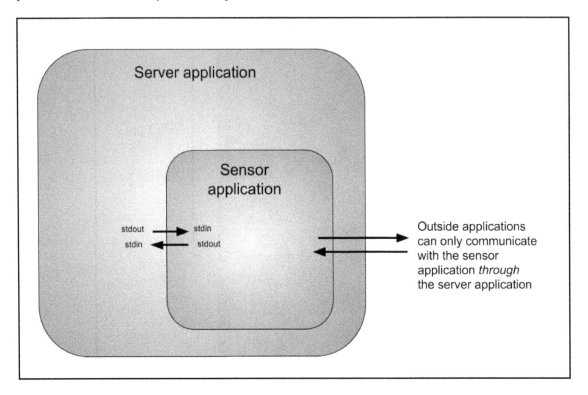

The downside of this is that the sensor service is entirely within the **Server application**, which means that any other application will not be able to make use of it unless the server allows it to (through its APIs).

If we want our sensor service to be available to other applications as well, an alternative approach is to have it occupy another port and communicate with other services through its own APIs:

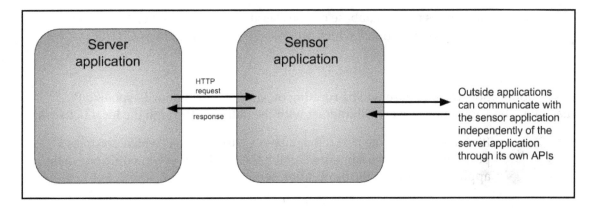

The **Sensor application** is now its own server. This way, it is now open to be reused by any other application through its APIs. The trade-off is that it takes additional resources and occupies another port. Additionally, it's much simpler to write a simple program that gives us output as **STDOUT** rather than a full-fledged server. In our application, we are going to use the first method because we only need to have the server communicating with the sensor, but you can expand into the second method if your architecture gets more complex.

The database - adding persistence to our data

Everything we have discussed until this point has been stateless. If we want to make use of data from another point in time or from other systems in a centralized way, we need to add a database.

By adding persistence, we add a lot of value to our application:

- We can now view values from the past
- We can now show changes in values rather than just the values themselves
- We can now store data from multiple sensors and view them together

Integrating the database into our application

The database is interfaced with the rest of the application through the server (yet another area where the server acts as the middleware). The server application will add, update, read, and delete data from the database through the use of queries.

All queries to the database can be classified under `Create`, `Read`, `Update`, or `Delete` operations, which are collectively referred to as **CRUD**.

In our application, the database will be running on another port in our Raspberry Pi machine. The application server will interact with the database through the local network.

 It's important to note that the database is also a server, which occupies a port. This is why we sometimes call it the database server, while our main application runs on the application server.

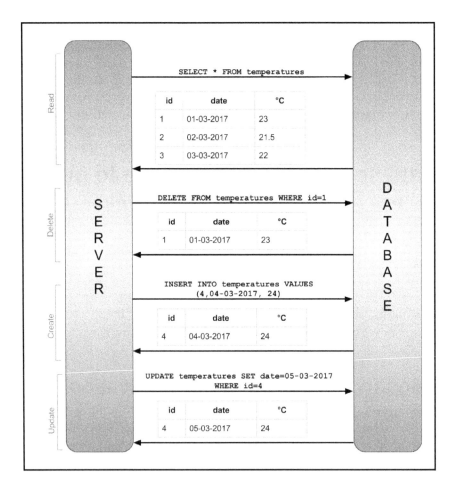

The overall architecture

Now that we have seen the interfaces between the different layers of the web development stack, we can visualize the overall architecture of the system:

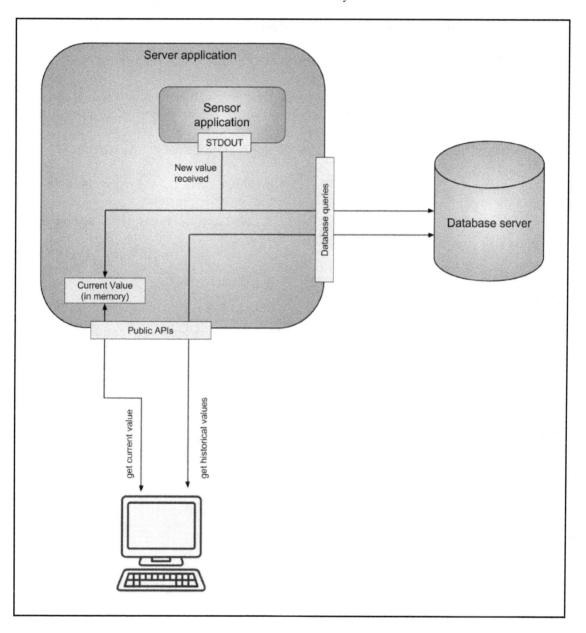

We can now see a high-level overview of all the components discussed so far. The interfaces between each layer discussed in the previous sections are now represented by the boundaries between each block in the diagram (**Public APIs**, **STDOUT**, and **Database queries**). The system will work as follows:

- The server application running on the Raspberry Pi interfaces with the rest of the components.
- It starts the program to get sensor values from the Pi and reads its output through **STDOUT**.
- Every time the server application receives a new value, it stores it in memory as well as in the database. The in-memory value is replaced every time a new value is received from the sensor.
- The client views and interacts with the application by calling APIs exposed by the server:
    - The API to get the current value returns the value that is currently stored in the memory of the server application
    - The API to get historical values has the server query the database and return its results

Summary

We looked at how computers, in general, connect and communicate with one another and also how different services running on a single computer can interact with one another on different ports. We then went on to discuss the different components of the web development stack and the different ways in which they could interact with each other and how they are useful in building our application. This included four main components: the server, sensor, database, and user interface. Finally, we were able to look at the high-level architecture made using all the concepts we discussed previously.

This chapter may have looked like it had a lot of theory, but an understanding of the big picture is very important before we move on to the details.

In the coming chapters, we will start with actually implementing each component we discussed here so that we can get our hands dirty.

3
Running a Node Server on the Pi

In the previous chapters, we discussed the different layers of the web application technology stack. One of these layers was the middleware layer, which plays an important role in coordinating all the other layers of our application. In order for our application to be robust and available, we must ensure that we use the right technology for the job. Node.js has proved to be a great fit for our use case. Its asynchronous nature matches our requirements of quick and uninterrupted communication between the different layers of our stack.

This chapter covers the basics of running a server application on your Raspberry Pi and includes the following:

- Installing the node on the Raspberry Pi
- The **node package manager** (**npm**) and library installation
- Deploying and running a node server on the Raspberry Pi

Introducing nodes - the server side JavaScript runtime

For anyone who is familiar with basic HTML development, JavaScript is a language restricted to the browser. For a long time, this was indeed the case, until 2009, when the first release of Node.js was written.

Node.js is a runtime for JavaScript, based on Chrome V8 engine, which allows JavaScript to run outside the browser. This gives it huge potential to do things it was never able to do inside the browser, such as:

- Reading and writing files on the system
- Binding to a port and running a server
- Making native system calls and interacting with other processes

We are eventually going to make use of all three of these functions to build our final application. Node has gained huge popularity both in the Enterprise and the IoT space because of its event-driven and non-blocking I/O model that makes it lightweight and efficient.

Installing node on the Pi

There are many ways to install node on the Raspberry Pi, but the easiest one is using the **Node Version Manager** (**nvm**), which is an open source node installer and version manager.

 From this point onward, all commands are executed on the Raspberry Pi, unless otherwise specified. To execute these commands, open the Raspberry Pi's Terminal either through SSH or by going to the desktop and opening the Terminal application.

First, install the `curl` command:

```
sudo apt-get update && sudo apt-get install curl
```

Then, install nvm via the install script:

```
curl -o-
https://raw.githubusercontent.com/creationix/nvm/v0.33.1/install.sh | bash
```

The preceding command installs the latest version of nvm at the time of writing this. If you would like to install a later version, replace `v0.33.1` in the URL with the latest version. Alternatively, you could see the complete installation command on nvms README page (h`ttps://github.com/creationix/nvm#install-script`). Once nvm is installed, verify its installation by running this:

```
nvm --version
```

It should give you the version number that has been installed.

Now that we have VM installed, the next step is to install the desired version of node. You can see the active version of the node on the official website (`https://nodejs.org`). Currently, version 6 is the active version under **Long Term Support** (**LTS**) and is recommended for most users. To install this version, run the command:

```
nvm install 6
```

nvm should now automatically install the node on your machine along with npm. Verify that the node and npm are installed:

```
pi@raspberrypi:~ $ node -v
v6.10.2
pi@raspberrypi:~ $ npm -v
3.10.10
```

The second and third numbers for each version may be different depending on the date of installation, but if all else is well, then you have successfully installed the node on your Raspberry Pi.

Running our first node program

Node is a JavaScript runtime, which means that it is an environment on top of which you can execute your JavaScript code. It is recommended that you make a new folder for all project files that we will use throughout this book.
Managing all the project files can be done with either of these ways:

- Using your favorite text editor application on the Raspberry Pi (if you are using the Raspberry Pi's desktop)
- Using one of the Terminal editors, such as vi or nano. This can be done on SSH or through the Raspberry Pi Terminal application.
- Editing files on a repository on your own computer and pushing changes to the Pi using a version control management tool like Git.

The last method is the most efficient and also the least error-prone. In fact, I feel it's appropriate to take a brief diversion to set it up so that we can work with a much clearer standard going forward:

Setting up a version control system

If you are familiar with maintaining projects remotely with version control systems such as Git or SVN, then you can skip this section. Version control systems make it easier to keep track of changes and also push and pull new versions of code from a remote repository. If you haven't already, install Git from `https://git-scm.com/`

Create a project folder and create a new Git repository inside your project folder (use the Terminal application for Mac and Linux or the Git bash program on Windows). The project folder will look like the one we made on our Raspberry Pi:

```
mkdir sensor-project
mkdir sensor-project/hello-world
touch sensor-project/hello-world/hello-world.js
cd sensor-project
git init
```

Add all your files to the repository and make a commit:

```
# Add all files to staging area
git add -A

# Commit to repository. Mark the commit with a message
git commit -m "Initialized first project"
```

Next, create a remote repository on a site such as GitHub (`https://github.com/`) or Bitbucket (`https://bitbucket.org/`)

You will get a remote URL (we can use `https://my-remote-repo-url.com/sensor-proje ct.git`for the purpose of this section):

```
# Add the remote link
git remote add origin https://my-remote-repo-url.com/sensor-project.git

# Push all changes to the remote repo
git push origin master
```

Now, all your code is present on the cloud. All you have to do now is go into your Raspberry Pi's Terminal and run this:

```
git clone https://my-remote-repo-url.com/sensor-project.git
cd ~/sensor-project
```

You now have the project fully cloned on your Pi. To make changes and reflect them on your Pi, first, make the changes to files or folders on your computer and then add and push the changes to the repository:

```
# Run these commands after making changes to code files
git add -A
git commit -m "Made some changes"
git push origin master
```

Then on your Pi, run this:

```
cd ~/sensor-project
git pull origin master
```

You now have version control set up and can easily push code from your machine to your Pi.

 The next time I mention "syncing code to the Pi" or "pushing code to the Pi", this pushing and pulling of code is what I'm referring to. If you are writing code directly on the Pi, you don't have to do this.

An interesting point to note is that since Git is decentralized, this process can also be done the other way round, which means that if you make any changes to the code on the Raspberry Pi and not on your local machine, you can push the code from your Pi and then pull it from your computer.

Back to our program

Let's pick up where we left off.

Open the hello-world.js file with your favorite text editor and modify its contents to this:

```
console.log('Hello World!');
```

Push your code to the Pi, then on your Pi's command line, inside the sensor-project folder, run this:

```
node hello-world/hello-world.js
```

You should see the Hello World! output printed to the console. Congratulations! You have just executed your first piece of server-side JavaScript code.

Installing external libraries

In theory, we could write all our code by ourselves, but it would be a long and difficult task. Fortunately for us, node comes bundled with npm, its own package manager. As the time of writing this, npm is the world's largest software registry. In this section, we are going to install some packages to make our development easier and less bug-prone.

Make a new folder inside the `sensor-project` folder and go into it:

```
mkdir server
cd server
```

When you're inside this folder, run the command:

```
npm init
```

npm will then take you through a series of prompts, which will look something like this:

```
pi@raspberrypi:~/sensor-project/server $ npm init
This utility will walk you through creating a package.json file.
It only covers the most common items, and tries to guess sensible defaults.

See `npm help json` for definitive documentation on these fields
and exactly what they do.

Use `npm install <pkg> --save` afterwards to install a package and
save it as a dependency in the package.json file.

Press ^C at any time to quit.
name: (server)
version: (1.0.0)
description: The server application for this project
entry point: (index.js)
test command:
git repository:
keywords:
author:
license: (ISC)
About to write to /home/pi/sensor-project/server/package.json:

{
  "name": "server",
  "version": "1.0.0",
  "description": "The server application for this project",
  "main": "index.js",
  "scripts": {
    "test": "echo \"Error: no test specified\" && exit 1"
  },
  "author": "",
  "license": "ISC"
}

Is this ok? (yes)
```

After this is done, you should see a package.json file at the root of the server directory. Install the express library by running this:

```
npm install --save express
```

npm will now fetch the express library from its registry and install it in the server folder. The --save flag indicates that we wish to update our package.json file, whose contents will now be as follows:

```
{
  "name": "server",
  "version": "1.0.0",
  "description": "The server application for this
project",
  "main": "index.js",
  "scripts": {
    "test": "echo \"Error: no test specified\" && exit 1"
  },
   "author": "",
  "license": "ISC",
  "dependencies": {
    "express": "^4.15.2"
  }
}
```

We can see express added under the dependencies object. This is because of the --save flag.

The package.json file provides all the metadata and information about a node project. It is generally present in the root directory of a project and contains information about a project, its repository, version, author, and dependent libraries required to be installed.

You will also see a node_modules folder. This folder contains the actual library code and data required for operation. This folder should not be included in our version control system because it can get pretty bulky, so create a .gitignore file and modify it to include this folder:

```
echo "node_modules" >> .gitignore
```

Developing the application server

Now that we have all the prerequisites set up, create an index.js file inside the root directory:

```
touch index.js
```

So far, we have created a lot of files and folders. Your sensor-project directory structure up until this point should look like this:

```
.
├── hello-world
│   └── hello-world.js
└── server
├── .gitignore
├── index.js
├── package.json
└── node_modules
└── ...
```

We are now going to write the code to run our server by editing the server/index.js file.

First, we have to import the express library we just installed:

```
const express = require('express');
```

The require function is a part of the node's standard library. It imports the module given as its argument and returns it. In this line, we are importing the express module and assigning it to the express variable.

 Whenever we require a node module, the node first checks the node_modules directory in the same directory where the file we are executing is present.

We then create an instance of a server application:

```
const app = express()
```

The express variable is a constructor, which is a function or method that returns an object. In our case, the express constructor returns an instance of an express server application.

Adding routes to the server

To create a good API server, we need to add HTTP endpoints, which will act as the interface between our server and the public. Let's define a simple route to get the temperature:

```
app.get('/temperature', function(req, res) {
  res.send('24 °C');
});
```

This code looks simple, but there's a lot going on here:

1. `app.get` is a method of the `app` server object, that when called, defines an HTTP GET endpoint.
2. `app.get` takes two arguments: the first one is the path, and the second one is the callback.
3. We define our path to be `/temperature`, which means that an HTTP client will have to make a GET request to `/temperature` in order to access this endpoint.
4. The `callback` is a function that is called every time the endpoint is hit. This function provides us with the `req` and `res` objects as arguments, which represent the request and response, respectively.
5. The `req` object gives us properties and methods of the request, while `res` gives us methods that enable us to send a response back to the client.
6. We are using the `res.send` method, which sends a simple text response back to the client when called, with the text to be sent being the first argument.

In short, we send a response of `'24 °C'` every time a GET request to `'/temperature'` is made.

We will also take a similar route for humidity:

```
app.get('/humidity', function(req, res) {
  res.send('48%');
});
```

Starting up the server

Now that we have defined our servers functionality, the only thing that's left to do is start it up:

```
app.listen(3000, function(){
  console.log('Server listening on port 3000');
});
```

1. The `listen` method of `app` is called, which starts up the server and has it listen on port `3000` of the Pi.
2. The first argument of `listen` is the port number we want to bind to.
3. The second argument is a `callback` function that is called once the server has started. Inside this `callback` function we output a message to the console to indicate that the server is up and running.

All the code combined will give you the final `server/index.js` file:

```
const express = require('express');
const app = express();

app.get('/temperature', function(req, res) {
  res.send('24 °C');
});

app.get('/humidity', function(req, res) {
  res.send('48%');
});

app.listen(3000, function(){
  console.log('Server listening on port 3000');
});
```

Push all code to the Pi, and from the root directory (`sensor-project`), run the command:

`node server`

And you will see this output:

If you noticed, we ran only `node server` and not `node server/index.js`, which is where our code actually is. This is because when you specify a folder name without a filename, the node automatically looks for an `index.js` file by convention. If you named your file something else, say, `index123.js`, you would not be able to do this and would have to write the full location: `node server/index123.js`

Now, open a browser on any computer connected to the network and go to the address `http://<raspbery_pis_ip_address>:3000/temperature`, and you will get the response of **24 °C**.

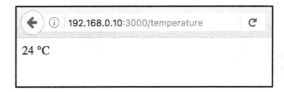

Similar is the case with `http://<raspbery_pis_ip_address>:3000/humidity`:

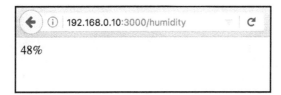

My Raspberry Pi's IP address, in this case, is `192.168.0.10`.

Keeping the server running in the background

We were able to successfully create and run our server in the previous section. However, if we close the Terminal or the SSH session with the Pi, our server will cease to exist as well. While this is okay in a development or testing setup, we would ideally want our server running in the background if we want to exit the Terminal session but still have access to our application.

This is where the `pm2` node module comes in. Just like `express`, `pm2` is also an npm library. This time, however, we will be installing it globally:

```
npm install -g pm2
```

The -g flag indicates that we want to install the pm2 module globally and not just in our project directory. What this will also do is install any binaries the module has as command-line tools.

 Install node modules globally if you want to use their command-line tools and if you want to use them across projects. Conversely, local node modules should be installed if you want to restrict their usage for only their project.

Verify that pm2 is installed by running this:

```
pm2 --version
```

If you are running pm2 for the first time, you should get a large output like this:

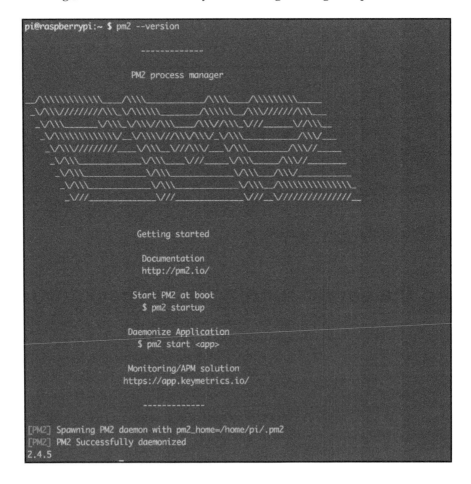

The last line gives you the version (at the time of writing this, it's 2.4.5), and the lines before that mention that pm2 has been demonized. This means that the pm2 process has been started and is running in the background.

We will use pm2 to run our application server in the background so that we can have it running even when we leave the Terminal session.

Inside your projects directory, run the command:

```
pm2 start server/
```

The pm2 will then start the node server in the background:

```
pi@raspberrypi:~/sensor-project $ pm2 start server/
[PM2] Starting /home/pi/sensor-project/server in fork_mode (1 instance)
[PM2] Done.

| App name | id | mode | pid  | status | restart | uptime | cpu | mem     | watching |
| server   | 0  | fork | 1944 | online | 0       | 0s     | 35% | 16.1 MB | disabled |

Use `pm2 show <id|name>` to get more details about an app
```

If you see this, that means that your server has now been started as a background process, and you can access it (via http://<raspbery_pis_ip_address>:3000/humidity or http://<raspbery_pis_ip_address>:3000/temperature) even if you leave the Terminal session (just don't turn off the Pi).

There is a lot more that pm2 has the capability to do. Just execute this:

```
pm2 --help
```

To know the full list of commands.

> Using the standard node command to start applications is preferred during development and testing, while using pm2 is better for when you are done with development and want your app running smoothly.

Summary

In this chapter, you learned about the Node.js runtime and its installation on the Raspberry Pi. Next, we made a brief diversion in order for you to learn how to sync our code between our own computers and the Pi using version control systems, such as Git. We then created and executed our first node program and went on to write a more complicated server program. In this process, we also explored npm and the installation of external libraries (node modules) using it. Lastly, you learned how to make a node process persistent using the pm2 library.

It is important to note that although we have covered a couple of node modules (such as express and pm2) in this chapter, the ecosystem is massive, and there are many other modules like these that can be used to make your life easier in many areas of software development. You can consider exploring https://www.npmjs.com/ to know some of the other popular packages that are out there.

In the next chapter, we will get closer to the metal by looking at how we can extract information from the GPIO pins to obtain real sensor information.

4
Extracting Information from the GPIO Pins

Throughout this book, you will be dealing with technology that is best suited for the Raspberry Pi but can also be somehow run in another environment, such as your laptop. Sure, the Raspberry Pi's portability plays a big role in its popularity in the IoT space, but the real value comes in its extraordinary interfacing ability through its GPIO pins. These pins can directly connect with most sensors and transmitters that you need in order to sense the outside world. Without these, the next best solution was to find another external facing development board or microcontroller (such as the Arduino) and communicate serially, which compromises both our portability and communication.

In this chapter, you will learn more about the GPIO pins and how to interface and communicate with them on our Raspberry Pi. We will also look at the DHT11 sensor module, which is a popular and low-cost sensor module used to measure the temperature and humidity of its surroundings. By the end of this chapter, you should be able to have your Pi give you the current temperature and humidity readings!

We will specifically cover the following topics:

- The GPIO pins on the Pi
- The pin as a standalone component
- Fine-tuning our control using the GPIO command-line tools
- The DHT11 sensor
- Reading from the sensor

The GPIO pins on the Pi

Each Pi (models **A+**, **B+**, **2B**, and **3B**) comes with a total of 40 pins. These can be either GPIO pins or they can have some other function, as shown in the following diagram:

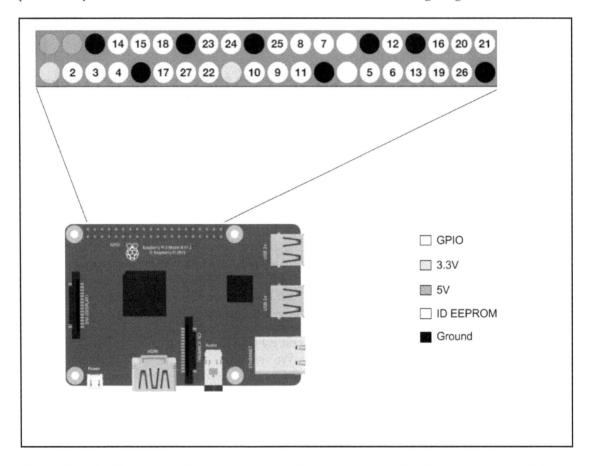

The **3.3V** and **5V** pins act only as a power supply and nothing else. We cannot control them with the Pi. Similarly, the ground pin acts as the negative terminal of this power supply. The GPIO pins are where all the action takes place since we can control them as well as read from them programmatically. The ID EEPROM pins are meant for more advanced usage and should not be manipulated unless you know exactly what you are doing.

The numbers on the pins may seem haphazard, and they are, but this is how the computer sees them. So when we refer to pin **2**, we are actually referring to the one numbered **2** in the previous diagram.

 Note that, throughout this book, the pin numbers we refer to are according to this diagram.

The pin as a standalone component

Let's take a deep dive and look at how exactly each GPIO pin on the Pi works. Each pin has two functions, which are what make up the IO in GPIO. Each pin can write binary values (and by values, what I mean is it can give an output between **0** and **3.3v**) and also read binary values.

The Write mode

In the **Write mode**, the Raspberry Pi acts as a switch and a power source.

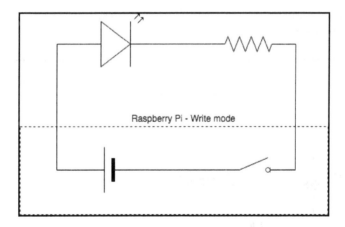

This diagram represents the `hello world` of circuits, that is, an LED along with a resistor connected to a power source. An important thing to remember is that any GPIO pin needs a reference, relative to which it can be high or low.

The Raspberry Pi can act as either end of this circuit and has two different ways of being an output pin based on the reference pin we use.

- The first configuration is when we use the ground pin as the reference pin.

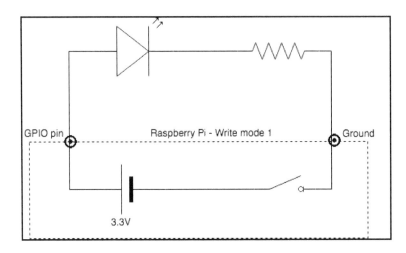

Here, the LED pin will glow when the **GPIO pin** is high relative to the ground pin and will be switched off when it is low.

- If you haven't guessed it already, the second configuration is when the **3.3V** pin is used as the reference:

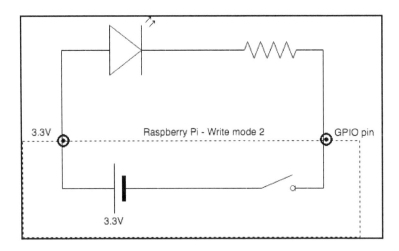

Here, the **GPIO pin** acts as the other side of this circuit. If it is set as high (**3.3V**), then the circuit will not have any current running through it and the LED would appear switched off. This is because the actual state of any circuit depends on the voltage difference and not the actual voltage on each Terminal. When we switch the **GPIO pin** to low, the voltage difference between the two ends now becomes **3.3v** and the LED starts glowing. Although this mode may seem awkward, it is useful in using the pin as an inverse switch (current flows when the pin is low as opposed to when it is high)

The Read mode

To better understand how the Raspberry Pi's GPIO pins are used as an input, let's use the same circuit as the one we used for its Write mode, with a notable exception: we will treat the Raspberry Pi as the combination of the battery and the LED.

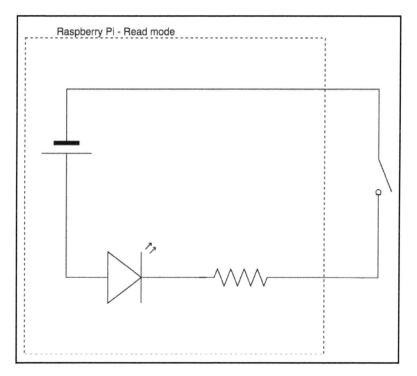

Here, the LED as the Pi is just a representation. There is no actual LED inside the Pi that will glow. We are just using it here as an illustration, where the LED glowing is analogous to the Pi reading a value of 1 and, similarly, the LED being switched off translates to the Pi reading a 0.

The battery is still a part of the Pi because even though the Pi is in **Read mode**, it needs a reference for its read operation. This means that any outside power source has to have the same reference level that the Pi is using, and this is normally done by connecting the ground pins of the Pi and the external power source.

Similar to Write mode, there are two configurations for **Read mode** of the GPIO pins:

- When we set the default value of the input pin to low, it is always low unless we give it a high input.

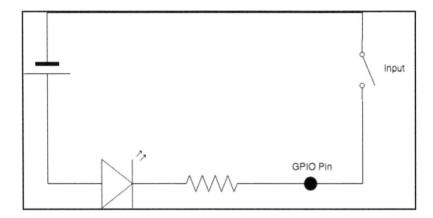

Here, the LED will glow when an input connects it to a high voltage; otherwise, it will not glow (which means the Pi will read low).

- When we set the pin to read in high mode, things can get a little non-obvious:

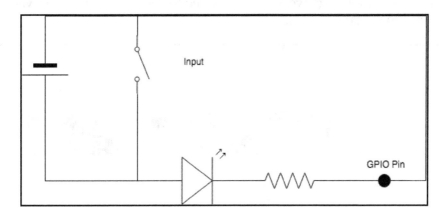

 If you do not have a background in electronics, just know that current flows through the path of least resistance, and a plain wire is supposed to have the least resistance as compared to any other electrical component.

We can see here that by default, the LED always glows because the circuit is complete. However, if there is an input that shorts the connection between the LED and the battery, the LED will stop glowing and the Pi will get a low reading.

Fine-tuning our control - using the GPIO command-line tools

Controlling the Raspberry Pi's GPIO pins is surprisingly simple using the GPIO command-line interface.

First, install the GPIO command-line tools by running this:

```
git clone git://git.drogon.net/wiringPi
cd wiringPi/
./build
```

Verify that the gpio command-line tool has been installed by running this:

```
gpio -v
```

Let's say we have an LED connected to pin **4** (to be more specific, the positive end is connected to pin **4** and the negative end is connected to one end of a resistor, whose other end is connected to the ground pin).

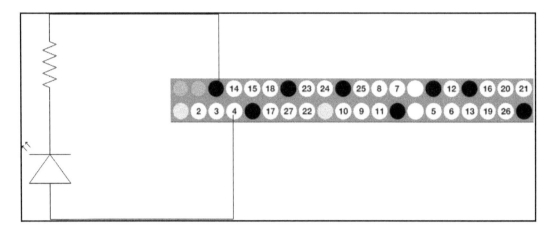

This circuit is similar to the pin-low Write mode we discussed earlier.

You can test this circuit through the following steps:

1. Set the pin 4 to output mode:

   gpio mode 4 output

2. Set the pin to high:

   gpio write 4 1

   You should now see the LED glowing.

3. Set the pin to low:

   gpio write 4 0

The LED should stop glowing now.

The GPIO command-line tools have many more features, such as pin reading, mode setting, and exporting. You can see a detailed view of all the features this tool has to offer on its main page:

man gpio

The DHT11 sensor

The external pins in the Raspberry Pi are great, but they don't offer much without a connection to the outside world. Another constraint that these pins have is that they cannot read analog values (such as the pins on an Arduino board). This means that each pin can read only a binary value.

Traditional sensors work by having a variable resistance, which changes with the quantity they want to measure. This, in turn, changes the current flowing through the circuit that can be measured by analog pins but not by the ones on the Pi.

We solve this problem using a digital sensor. These sensors work by giving us information in the form of bits at a fixed sampling rate. This is where the DHT11 sensor comes in. It is a low-cost digital temperature and humidity sensor. It has four pins, out of which three will be of use to us.

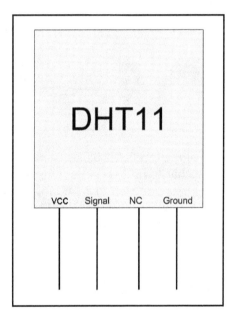

If you purchase a DHT11 sensor in the form of a printed circuit board, the names of these pins will also clearly be present next to the pins:

- **VCC** is connected to the power supply, which is the 5V pin in our case
- **Ground** is connected to the Pi's ground pin

- Signal is connected to a GPIO pin. For this example, let's connect it to pin 4.
- **NC** is an auxiliary pin and is not used

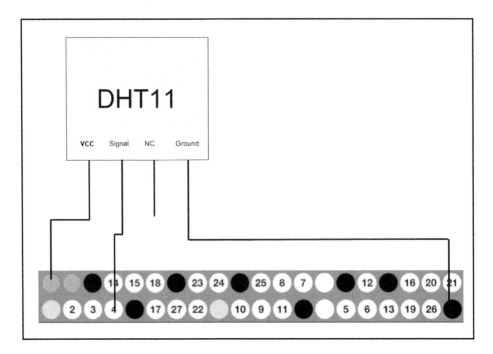

 The sampling rate of the DHT11 is 0.5Hz, which means the minimum time in between readings has to be 2 seconds. This is one of the trade-offs to using a digital sensor as opposed to an analog sensor. Analog sensors readings are real time, while with the DHT11, we will get a minimum lag of 2 seconds, which is acceptable for our use case.

Reading from the sensor

Now that everything's connected, let's take a reading from our sensor. The DHT11 sensor gives us a 40-bit reading over the time span of 2 seconds. Timing and reading each bit can be a complex task. Fortunately for us, there are libraries present to make our lives easier.

Node.js does not have the required support for the DHT11 sensor, and we need to install the `bcm2835` library in order to interface with the sensor.

To install the library, run the following commands:

```
wget http://www.airspayce.com/mikem/bcm2835/bcm2835-1.52.tar.gz
tar -xvzf bcm2835-1.52.tar.gz
cd bcm2835-1.52
./configure
make
sudo make check
sudo make install
```

Next, go to the `~/sensor-project/server` directory and create a new file called `obtain-readings.js`.

Install the `node-dht-sensor` library:

```
npm install --save node-dht-sensor
```

Populate the contents of the `obtain-readings.js` file:

```
//Import the sensor library
const sensor = require('node-dht-sensor')

//The first argument is the sensor number. In this case
 11 represents the DHT11 sensor
//The second argument is the pin number to read from, for
this example, we have connected
//the signal pin to pin 4
 sensor.read(11, 4, function(err, temperature, humidity)
{
    //After reading the sensor, we get the temperature
and humidity readings
    if (!err) {
        //If there is no error, log the readings to the
console
        console.log('temp: ' + temperature.toFixed(1) +
 '°C, ' +
            'humidity: ' + humidity.toFixed(1) + '%'
        )
    }
});
```

Run this file, and you should see the temperature and humidity readings showing up:

```
pi@raspberrypi:~/sensor-project/server $ node obtain-reading.js
temp: 25.0°C, humidity: 70.0%
pi@raspberrypi:~/sensor-project/server $
```

Summary

In this chapter, we went deep into the hardware of our Pi. You learned about the GPIO pin configuration and took a detailed look at how they work in the Read mode as well as the Write mode. Next, we went on to learn how to fine-tune our control over the GPIO pins using the `gpio` command-line utility.

Finally, we looked at the DHT11 sensor to measure temperature and humidity. We used a supporting C library so that our `node` code could interface with the sensor and finally wrote a program in JavaScript that printed the temperature and humidity readings to the console.

Our Raspberry Pi now has some sensory capability and has the data it needs to be an IoT device. In the next chapter, you will learn how to expose our sensor readings to the public by integrating with the node server we built in the previous chapter.

5
Retrieving Sensor Readings from the Server

In the previous chapter, we managed to get hands-on with interfacing our sensors with the Raspberry Pi's GPIO pins and were able to get the temperature and humidity readings of the surroundings. However, we still require a way to get this information to our users. After all, information is useless if nobody can see it. Another interesting concept that we saw was that our sensor was digital and not analog, which meant that it sent us information in the form of multiple bits at a regular interval, as opposed to analog sensors whose current we can read in real time. While the interval in which our sensor takes reading is more or less real time, it poses unique problems when we couple it with on-demand readings.

In this chapter, you will learn how to integrate our sensor readings, which we obtained in Chapter 4, *Extracting Information from the GPIO Pins*, with the node server that we developed in Chapter 3, *Running a Node Server on the Pi*. We will also look at some of the complexities involved with our sensor and the way it takes readings at fixed intervals and you will learn how to resolve them using function memoization patterns.

Understanding how our node process takes readings

In order to integrate our sensor reading code into our server, first. let's understand what is happening under the hood whenever we execute the node script that takes our sensor readings. Let's review the snippet of code that actually called for the sensor readings:

```
/*
Section A
*/
sensor.read(11, 4, function(err, temperature, humidity) {
    /*
    Section B
    */
    //After reading the sensor, we get the temperature
and humidity readings
    if (!err) {
        //If there is no error, log the readings to the
console
        console.log('temp: ' + temperature.toFixed(1) +
'°C, ' +
            'humidity: ' + humidity.toFixed(1) + '%'
        )
    }
});
/*
Section C
*/
```

Immediately, we can see that the `sensor.read` method is not synchronous; that is, it does not immediately return the result upon invocation. This is because it isn't actually the node script that obtains the readings from the pin. Rather, it makes use of a third-party library that runs native code to do this (this is the `bcm2835` C library that we installed in the previous chapter). This native code, on running and producing results, then passes it back to our node process, which can run further processing.

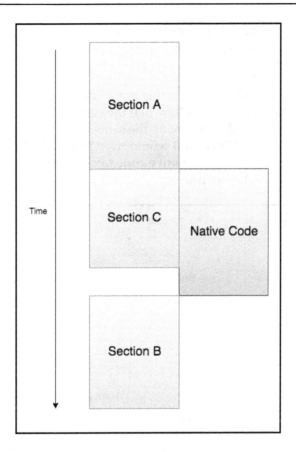

As we can see from the preceding timing diagram, **Section A** calls the native library to execute some instructions, which, in our case, is obtaining readings from the sensor pins. Node.js executes this operation asynchronously, which means that it does not wait for the native code to return our results to us and moves on with code execution. This means that any code written outside the callback will be executed while the node process waits for the native process to return our results to us.

Finally, after the sensor readings are made available by the native library, the code inside the `callback` (**Section B**) is called.

 The asynchronous model is an important pattern to understand, as it is what makes the node so appealing in the first place. The model described here is also used in database operations and server requests and is the default way that node handles I/O.

An interesting piece of information to note is that the node works on the basis of `event` loops, which are functions, or pieces of code, that get pushed into the queue and are executed one after the other.

Node is also single threaded, which means that any of these pieces of code cannot be executed at the same time. Although we saw that the native code and **Section C** were executed together, the native code was not on the same thread as the node process. What this can potentially mean is that **Section B** would have to wait for **Section C** to finish its execution before it executes (even if the native code fetches results sooner) because Section C was pushed into the queue before it was.

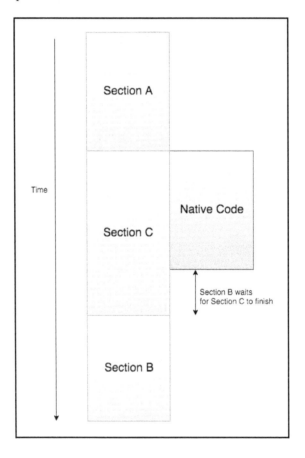

Modifying our server code to show sensor readings

In Chapter 3, *Running a Node Server on the Pi*, we developed a node server that had APIs to obtain the temperature and humidity. We did not return real data but used a mock hardcoded response to give the impression of real data. In this section, we will be integrating the code that we discussed in Chapter 4, *Extracting Information from the GPIO Pins*, and including it in our server code so that every time you make a request to the temperature and humidity APIs, you get real, live data.

Let's take the example of the temperature API:

```
app.get('/temperature', function(req, res) {
  res.send('24 °C');
});
```

Now, we add the code for reading from the sensor inside this API:

```
app.get('/temperature', function (req, res) {
  sensor.read(11, 4, function (err, temperature,
humidity) {
    if (err) {
      console.error(err);
    }
    res.send(temperature.toFixed(1) + '°C');
  });
});
```

We call the `sensor.read` method every time a user makes a request to `/temperature`.

Note that we send the response inside the `callback` of the `sensor.read` method. This is because we want to wait until the sensor has returned its readings before we send anything back to the user.

We similarly modify the humidity API and get the resulting `server.js` file:

```
const express = require('express');
const app = express();
const sensor = require('node-dht-sensor');

app.get('/temperature', function (req, res) {
  sensor.read(11, 4, function (err, temperature,
humidity) {
    if (!err) {
      res.send(temperature.toFixed(1) + '°C');
```

```
    }
  });
});

app.get('/humidity', function (req, res) {
  sensor.read(11, 4, function (err, temperature,
humidity) {
    if (!err) {
      res.send(humidity.toFixed(1) + '%');
    }
  });
});

app.listen(3000, function(){
  console.log('Server listening on port 3000');
});
```

Overall, our servers, architecture can be described in terms of this diagram:

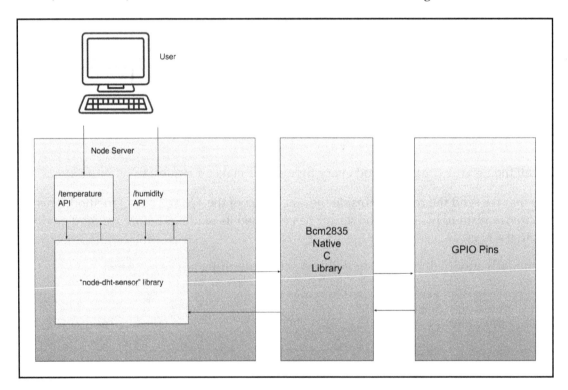

Optimizing our server

So it looks like we got our server working with the sensor readings and everything... great! However, there are a few issues with our implementation that we need to handle. Looking at the server code from the previous example, we can note the following points:

- We are repeating a lot of code; not only does this make our code look bad, but it also makes it less malleable. What if we want to change our sensor pin number from 4 to 6? We need to change the code in two places. Even worse, what if we decide to change the sensor or even the way in which we get sensor readings in the future?

- We are making calls to the native library every time someone hits the API. This is fine when we are testing it on our local machine, but what if we had multiple users hitting our API at the same time? It is highly inefficient to make so many calls to the native library, especially if the information we are getting is going to be the same. (If you recall, our sensor's sampling rate is one in every 2 seconds).

- We are obtaining unneeded information. The sensor gives us readings for both the temperature and humidity at the same time (by design). The way we have separated our APIs for temperature and humidity means that we do not require the humidity information in the temperature API and vice versa.

Fortunately, all three problems are resolvable. Let's tackle them one at a time.

Abstracting our sensor library code

We made three assumptions in our previous example:

- We will always use the DHT11 sensor
- The sensor will always be attached to pin 4
- We will always use the `node-dht-sensor` library

Unfortunately, it isn't wise to assume that these assumptions will always hold true because of the following reasons:

- We may opt for the more accurate DHT22 sensor
- Pin 4 may get fried, after which we will have to switch to a different pin
- The `node-dht-sensor` library may become deprecated in favor of a more up-to-date library

In any case, as developers, we should make sure that our code remains as flexible as possible. To do this, one possible solution is to make a separate file dedicated to retrieving our sensor readings:

```
const sensor = require('node-dht-sensor')
/*
We abstract away the functionality to read sensor
information inside the getSensorReadings function.
This function is also asynchronous. It accepts a callback
function as an argument.
*/
const getSensorReadings = (callback) => {
    sensor.read(11, 4, function (err, temperature,
 humidity) {
        if (err) {
          /*
          If there is an error, call the callback function
with the error as its first argument
          */
          return callback(err)
        }
        /*
        If everything went well, call the callback with
"null" as the first argument to indicate that there was
no error.
        The second and third arguments would be the results
(temperature and humidity respectively)
        */
        callback(null, temperature, humidity)
    })
}

/*
Finally, export the function so that it can be used by
other parts of our code
*/
module.exports = getSensorReadings
```

Now that we have separated the sensor read process in a separate module, let's refactor our server code to use it:

```
const express = require('express')
const app = express()
const getSensorReadings = require('./get-sensor-
readings')

app.get('/temperature', function (req, res) {
  getSensorReadings((err, temperature, humidity) => {
```

```
      if (!err) {
        res.send(temperature.toFixed(1) + '°C')
      }
    })
  })

  app.get('/humidity', function (req, res) {
    getSensorReadings((err, temperature, humidity) => {
      if (!err) {
        res.send(humidity.toFixed(1) + '%')
      }
    })
  }

  app.listen(3000, function () {
    console.log('Server listening on port 3000')
  })
```

Now, we can change the way we get sensor readings and still have our server working fine as long as we follow the `callback` signature.

Caching our results

Our next problem is that we do not want to actually call our sensor interface every time someone requests the temperature and humidity through our API. To solve this, we need to cache our results.

In simple terms, this means that we need a temporary form of storage for the latest results. Whenever we receive a request, we will return results from this temporary storage, and not call the native sensor interface. In the background, we will periodically (the same period as the sensor) obtain readings from the sensor and update the cache.

Caching our results also provides us with other benefits:

- Our server becomes much faster since the results are obtained directly from local memory rather than having to be read from the native interface, whose I/O operations could slow down the response time considerably.
- As far as the server is concerned, the operation for fetching temperature and humidity becomes synchronous. This makes it much more straightforward and easier to deal with. You will observe this once you take a look at the modified server code.

- It provides us with a fail-safe way if there is any error. In case something goes wrong and the sensor is not able to receive readings, we can still use the latest values that were stored in the cache.

```
const getSensorReadings = require('./get-sensor-
readings')

/*
Instantiate the cache. In this case its a simple variable
stored in local memory
*/
const cache =
  temperature: null,
  humidity: null
}

/*
Run a function to get the sensor readings every 2 seconds
(the same sampling rate as our sensor)
*/
setInterval(() => {
  getSensorReadings((err, temperature, humidity) => {
    if (err) {
      return console.error(err)
    }
    /*
    Set the values of the cache on receiving new readings
    */
    cache.temperature = temperature
    cache.humidity = humidity
  })
}, 2000)

/*
The functions that we expose only return the cached
values, and don't make a call to the sensor interface
everytime
*/
module.exports.getTemperature = () => cache.temperature
module.exports.getHumidity = () => cache.humidity
```

Something you may have noticed is that we initialize our cache with `const` even though we change its properties' values later. This is because `const` in JavaScript ES6 standard refers only to a constant assignment and not a constant value. Even though we change the values of the temperature and humidity properties of the cache variable, we do not reassign the variable itself.

Another thing you may have noticed is that we are already reaping the benefits of abstracting our sensor reading code. The cache module does not have any idea of how we are retrieving our temperature and humidity and leaves that functionality to the `get-sensor-readings` module

Let's modify our server code to use this new implementation:

```
const express = require('express')
const app = express()
const getCachedSensorReadings = require('./get-cached-
sensor-readings')

/*
We now utilize the synchronous methods exported from the
'get-cached-sensor-readings' module
*/
app.get('/temperature', function (req, res) {
res.send(getCachedSensorReadings
.getTemperature().toFixed(1) + '°C')
})

app.get('/humidity', function (req, res) {
  res.send(getCachedSensorReadings
.getHumidity().toFixed(1) + '%')
})

app.listen(3000, function () {
  console.log('Server listening on port 3000')
})
```

By doing this, we have now solved the second and third problems, namely:

- The requests to the server do not make calls to the native interface anymore; rather, they get that information from the cache
- We have separated the logic to retrieve temperature and humidity

The architecture diagram after these modifications will look like this:

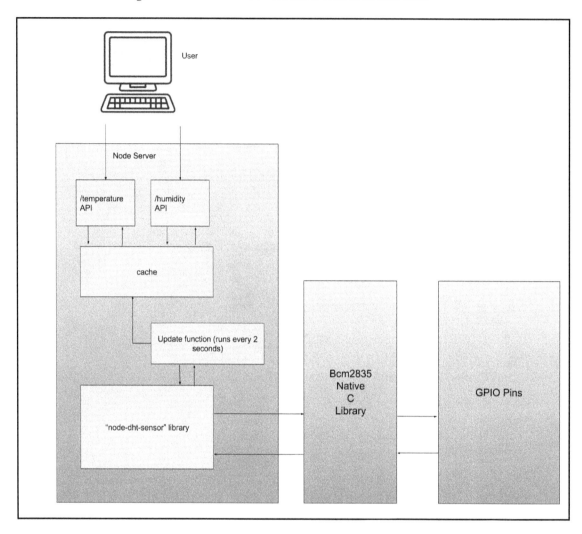

Although caching sounds like a silver bullet, we must also consider some of the trade-offs that we are making when we implement this approach:

- The initial readings are not available. For a short time period before the first reading gets stored into the cache, the values of the temperature and humidity are null. All users hitting our API at this time would see this null reading.
- Error handling becomes more difficult. In our previous implementation, we could send the error back to the user or log it whenever something went wrong. Now, since the fetching of readings is decoupled from the API responses, it's difficult from the frontend to ascertain whether something has gone wrong.

It is possible to solve both these problems, but for our use case, they are irrelevant. This is because we know that the time to fetch the reading is small (2 seconds), and even though we are not sending any errors back to the frontend, we are logging them as and when they occur.

By now, you should have a fully working application, in the sense that a user can type a URL into a browser and receive live information about the temperature and humidity:

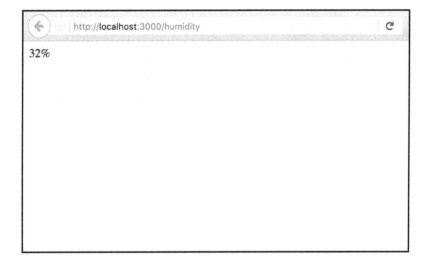

Summary

This chapter was the glue between the last two chapters. We began the chapter by taking a deep dive into how our node server communicates with native libraries. You learned about the asynchronous model that node uses to make I/O operations more efficient. This model is important to understand because it will also carry forward to the coming chapters.

We proceeded to integrate the sensor API from the previous chapter with our node server, and then we went on to see some of its limitations due to the hardware and sampling rate. Caching turned out to be a convenient and effective way to get around these limitations. The kind of local memory caching used in this chapter, however, would not be effective in a system that has multiple Raspberry Pi systems and sensors working together. In the upcoming chapters, you will learn about a more production-grade model to store and read our data.

Although we have a working application, our work is not done yet. Our application, in its current state, seems like it's more suitable for computers compared to humans. This is not something a user of your application would be delighted to see.

It's rather.... plain. As a user, I want a more intuitive way to see my information and not plain text in the corner of my screen.

In the next chapter, you will learn how to solve this problem by building a UI to present the information we have in a more consumable way to humans. This does not mean that the APIs we built will go to waste. In fact, we are going to make use of these APIs to retrieve the information that we present to the user.

6
Creating a Web Page to Display Sensor Data

Up until now, we have been dealing primarily with data and backend code, something that is almost completely invisible to the end user of our application. We did display some data, but this was only plain text and was unintuitive for the user to see. Furthermore, we had separate URLs in order to view temperature and humidity readings. This is not the ideal experience and can be made much better.

In this chapter, we will be looking at the presentation layer, otherwise known as the UI, and use web technologies to functionally and visually enhance the user experience. First, we will look at how to extend our current application to deliver HTML to the user instead of standard plain text. We will then look at how to display temperature and humidity at the same time using different APIs. We will also look at how to add dynamic style to our page to make it more visually appealing.

We will cover the following topics in this chapter:

- Extending our application
- Building the UI's functionality
- Visually enhancing the UI

Extending our application

The first step in enhancing our application is to have it deliver HTML instead of plain text. HTML is the markup language of the web, which is used to give a web page its structure. In essence, it's just a bunch of tags that give meaning to the text.

For example, the current output from the temperature API is `26°C`. Although it gives us the information we need, it would be more meaningful to highlight the actual value more than the unit. An output of `26°C` looks better than our plain text version.

Let's translate this into HTML. We have the strong tag, which is used to give emphasis to the text by making it thicker than usual.

The standard format of HTML tags is as follows:

```
<tag>text</tag>
```

Here, we replace `tag` with the name of our `tag`. If we wanted to make only the value bolder, we would write this:

```
<strong>26</strong> °C
```

The good news is that our node server can already deliver this. When plain text contains HTML tags, almost all popular browsers automatically treat it as HTML.

We will then modify our temperature API to highlight the value of the temperature:

```
app.get('/temperature', function (req, res) {
   res.send('<strong>' +
getCachedSensorReadings.getTemperature().toFixed(1) +
     '</strong>' + '°C')
})
```

Try hitting this URL in your browser, and you should see the temperature value in bold.

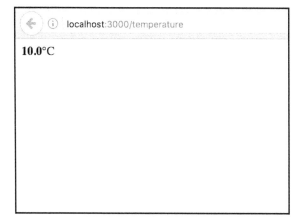

Serving static files from the Express server

While the previous example will work for simple enhancements, it will be difficult and inconvenient to embed an entire HTML web page in a string. A better way to go about it is to make an `index.html` file, which we can then serve from a different route. In the same directory as your `index.js` file, create another file called `index.html`:

```
<!DOCTYPE html>
<html lang="en">
  <head>
    <title>Sensor monitoring dashboard</title>
  </head>
  <body>
  <p><strong>10</strong> °C</p>
  </body>
</html>
```

The seventh line in the preceding file is the one we are actually interested in. Everything else is standard HTML5 boilerplate and metadata.

Note that at this point, we have not made a connection between the HTML document and the actual data coming from our server. We will come back to this later in the chapter. Also, the name `index.html` is the default name for the entry point into any frontend web application.

Now that we have our HTML file in place, we need to serve it from our server. Let's add another route to serve our HTML file:

```
app.get('/public', function (req, res) {
  res.sendFile(path.join(__dirname, 'index.html'))
})
```

Your `server.js` file should now look like this:

```
const express = require('express')
const path = require('path')
const app = express()
const getCachedSensorReadings = require('./get-
cached-
sensor-readings')

app.get('/temperature', function (req, res) {
    res.send('<strong>' +
getCachedSensorReadings.getTemperature()
.toFixed(1) +
  '</strong>' + '°C')
})
```

```
app.get('/humidity', function (req, res) {
    res.send(getCachedSensorReadings.getHumidity()
.toFixed(1) + '%')
})

 app.get('/public', function (req, res) {
  res.sendFile(path.join(__dirname, 'index.html'))
})

app.listen(3000, function () {
    console.log('Server listening on port 3000')
})
```

Run this file with node and navigate to `http://<raspberry-pi-ip>:3000/public`, and you should see the same output as the previous section. The difference here is that it is served from a file, as opposed to directly sending a string as the API response.

Going forward, the `index.html` file is not the only one we are going to have. We will eventually have script files and style sheets as well. This leads to a couple of problems:

- Making different APIs to serve each one of them can be time-consuming
- The code file structure can get confusing since our frontend and backend files would get mixed in the same folder

We can solve both these problems by making another directory just for our frontend assets and serving all files inside that directory. Fortunately for us, Express supports this out of the box.

Inside the current folder, create another directory called `public` and place the `index.html` file inside of it.

Your directory will now look like this:

```
.
├── get-cached-sensor-readings.js
├── get-sensor-readings.js
├── index.js
└── public
└── index.html
```

Next, modify the index.js server file to remove the public route and add the Express static middleware:

```
const express = require('express')
const path = require('path')
const app = express()
const getCachedSensorReadings = require('./get-cached-
sensor-readings.1')

/*
Here, we are introduced to express middleware.
Middleware is a fancy word to describe a set of actions
that have to take place before the request handler.

In the below statement, we use the express.static
middleware, and bind it to the /public route.
*/
app.use('/public', express.static(path.join(__dirname,
'public')))

app.get('/temperature', function (req, res) {
  res.send('<strong>' +
getCachedSensorReadings.getTemperature().toFixed(1) +
'</strong>' + '°C')
})

app.get('/humidity', function (req, res) {
  res.send(getCachedSensorReadings.getHumidity
().toFixed(1) + '%')
})

app.listen(3000, function () {
  console.log('Server listening on port 3000')
})
```

Again, once you open the /public route on your browser, you will see the same result as the last two times. However, what we have done here is made room for more files in the future (and by future, I mean the next section of this chapter).

Building the UI's functionality

Now that we have extended our server-side code to support the client-side file server, we can enhance the current web page (which is just some static data at this point) and give it the functionality it needs to pull data from the server.

Adding client-side JavaScript

In the third chapter, we started work with Node.js, which was JavaScript that ran on the server side. Now, we're going to introduce client-side JavaScript, or JavaScript that runs on the browser.

To run JavaScript on the browser, you will need to add a script tag anywhere in the HTML document.

The standard script tag looks like this:

```
<script>
console.log('Executing client side javascript ...')
</script>
```

It is better, however, to put your JavaScript code in a separate file altogether, which is when you would use the alternate syntax:

```
<script src="script.js"></script>
```

Add this script tag as the last element inside `<body>`.
Along with this, include a file called `script.js` in the `public` directory and populate its contents with this:

```
console.log('Executing client side javascript...')
```

Open your browser and open its console (commonly opened by right-clicking anywhere and going to the **Inspect** element. Here's how it looks when run on Firefox:

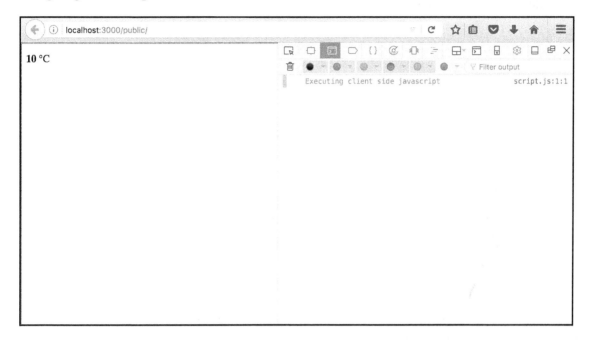

Even though you can add JavaScript anywhere in the document, it is recommended that you have it as the last element in your HTML body. This is because the document is rendered synchronously, and any JavaScript present is executed before the rest of the document is loaded. Putting the JavaScript in the end ensures that your users do not see the document getting stuck half way.

Fetching sensor readings using XHR

Earlier, we were retrieving sensor readings by directly navigating to the APIs locations. In this section, we are going to use client-side JavaScript to asynchronously fetch results from the same APIs and display it on our page.

We will be using the `fetch` API for this purpose. The `fetch` API is supported on almost all browsers except IE and Opera mini (you can find the complete support table here: `https://caniuse.com/#feat=fetch`).

Let's jump right in and use the fetch API to get the temperature readings from our server.

Include the following code in your client-side `script.js` file:

```
/*
 The fetch API uses a promise based syntax. It may look a
little weird if you're seeing it for the first time, but
it's an improvement over callbacks.
*/

/*
First, we instantiate the first promise, which call the
API at /temperature of our server
*/
fetch('/temperature')
.then(results => {
  /*
  results.text() returns another promise, which resolves
to the text response we receive from the API
  */
  return results.text()
})
.then(text => {
  /*
   This "text" variable is the response that the server
gives us. Logging it on the console will show you "
  <strong>10.0</strong>°C"
  */
  console.log(text)
})
```

We have now seen how to get the results on to the console, but what we actually want is to have the results on our UI.

Modify the `p` element in your HTML and give it an ID of `temperature-display`. Also, put a default message to be shown before the results are fetched:

```
<p id="temperature-display">Loading temperature...</p>
```

Now, we will add the following code in place of the `console.log`(text), which was there inside the second promise `callback` earlier:

```
const temperatureDisplay =
document.getElementById('temperature-display')
temperatureDisplay.innerHTML = text
```

The final `script.js` file will look like this:

```
fetch('/temperature')
.then(results => {
  return results.text()
})
.then(text => {
  /*
  Get the 'p' element as a variable, and set its inner
HTML to the response we received from the server
  */
  const temperatureDisplay =
document.getElementById('temperature-display')
  temperatureDisplay.innerHTML = text
})
```

When you refresh your browser to reflect the new files, you should see the actual temperature reading from the server instead of the hardcoded one we put in the beginning of this chapter.

We need to do two more things before we move on to the next section:

1. Separate the preceding code into its own function. This is because we will need to call this function at a regular interval in order to reflect updates in the temperature.
2. Replicate this logic for the humidity API.

Modify the `index.html` file to have another slot for humidity and label both of them for the sake of clarity:

```
<!DOCTYPE html>
<html lang="en">

<head>
  <title></title>
  <meta charset="UTF-8">
  <meta name="viewport" content="width=device-width,
initial-scale=1">
  <!--<link href="css/style.css" rel="stylesheet">-->
</head>

<body>
  <p>Temperature :</p>
  <p id="temperature-display">Loading temperature...</p>
  <p>Humidity :</p>
  <p id="humidity-display">Loading humidity...</p>
  <script src="script.js"></script>
```

```
</body>

</html>
```

Modify the `script.js` file to fetch information at a regular interval and add a similar functionality for the humidity:

```
/*
We put the code for fetching temperature in its own
function
*/
const fetchTemperature = () => {
  fetch('/temperature')
    .then(results => {
      return results.text()
    })
    .then(text => {
      const temperatureDisplay =
document.getElementById('temperature-display')
      temperatureDisplay.innerHTML = text
    })
}

/*
Make a similar function to fetch humidity
*/
const fetchHumidity = () => {
  fetch('/humidity')
    .then(results => {
      return results.text()
    })
    .then(text => {
      const temperatureDisplay =
document.getElementById('humidity-display')
      temperatureDisplay.innerHTML = text
    })
}

/*
Call the above defined functions at regular intervals
*/
setInterval(() => {
  fetchTemperature()
  fetchHumidity()
}, 2000)
```

We also have to make a change to the humidity API in the `server.js` file so that it too gives us the humidity in bold:

```
app.get('/humidity', function (req, res) {
   res.send('<strong>' +
getCachedSensorReadings.getHumidity().toFixed(1) +
   '</strong>' + '%')
})
```

Reload the server and open your browser, and you should now see the temperature and humidity readings changing at regular intervals, with actual readings from the sensor. Neat!

Visually enhancing the UI

Our UI works, and we have `async` XHR calls going for us, but it still feels like something is missing, probably because our UI just looks very plain:

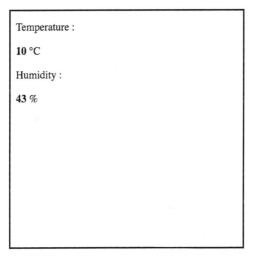

In this section, we will use HTML and CSS to make it look a lot better. We will also establish a layout structure that we can then use through out the next chapters as well.

When deciding a layout for the applications UI, it's always better to make a rough structure before you jump into coding:

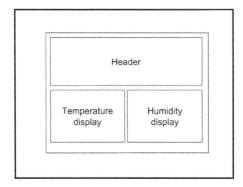

Our overall application will have a title bar and two displays to display the temperature and humidity.

We can drill-down into the details of each display:

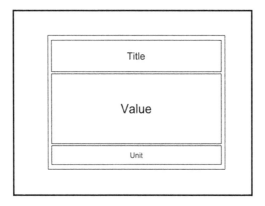

- We want each sensor display to show the physical quantity that it is measuring, its value, and its unit.
- We want to emphasize the value of the reading more than anything else, so we make it the largest.
  - The quantity and unit are more or less fixed and, therefore, do not provide much information to the user. We will make these fields smaller in size.

Now that we have our design finalized, let's get down to the implementation.

Changing the structure of our UI

First, we modify the structure of our UI to reflect the design we decided in the previous section:

```html
<!DOCTYPE html>
<html lang="en">

<head>
  <title></title>
  <meta charset="UTF-8">
  <meta name="viewport" content="width=device-width,
initial-scale=1">
  <!--The stylesheet is added here. We haven't made it
yet, so don't worry if you get an error at this point-->
  <link href="style.css" rel="stylesheet">
</head>

<body>
  <!--
    This is our "Title" element. It will occupy the
entire top band of our application
  -->
  <header>Sensor Dashboard</header>

  <!--
    We make a container structure to encapsulate our
temperature and humidity displays
  -->
  <div class="container">

    <!--
      Here, we define the structure of each display
    -->
    <div class="temperature">
      <!--
        Add subsections for the title, value, and unit.
        We give each section a class name, because we
want to style each one differently (give a larger size to
value as opposed to title and unit)
      -->
      <p class="title">Temperature</p>
      <p class="value" id="temperature-
display">Loading... </p>
      <p class="unit" >°C</p>
    </div>

    <!--
```

```
        The humidity display has a similar structure to the
temperature display
    -->
    <div class="humidity">
      <p class="title">Humidity</p>
      <p class="value" id="humidity-display">Loading...
</p>
      <p class="unit" >°C</p>
    </div>

  </div>
  <script src="script.js"></script>
</body>

</html>
```

Now that we have separated value from unit, we should change our server response to only send us the value.

 We will eventually move on to JSON responses; this is just an intermediate step.

```
app.get('/temperature', function (req, res) {
  res.send('<strong>' +
getCachedSensorReadings.getTemperature().toFixed(1) +
 '</strong>')
})

app.get('/humidity', function (req, res) {
   res.send('<strong>' +
getCachedSensorReadings.getHumidity().toFixed(1) +
 '</strong>')
})
```

Adding style to the newly modified structure

Style (by which I mean color, sizing, shadows, and all the other good stuff) is added to our newly structured layout with the help of CSS (or more specifically, CSS3). First, create a new file called `style.css` in the public directory. The HTML file already has the tag to include this CSS file:

```
<link href="style.css" rel="stylesheet">
```

The CSS file contains declarations that describe the style of the HTML elements in our document:

```
/*
Initialize the body to have no padding and margin so that
our aplication can occupy the entire screen
*/
body{
  margin:0;
  padding: 0;
}

/*
We use flexbox for our layout structure.
Flexbox is a feature introduced in CSS3 to make it
simpler to align
and size elements in a layout. It also makes your layout
more predictable
when accomodating different screen sizes.
*/
.container {
  display: flex;
  font-family : sans-serif;
  width: 100%;
}

/*
Assign a width to the containers. Since we have two
 containers,
and we want there to be space in between, we need to make
each of them
lesser than 50% of the total width, which is why 40% is
assigned.

The top and bottom margin is set at 20px, while the left
and right margins are
set to auto, so that both containers will center
themselves.

We also want the text inside these containers to align
 itself centrally
*/
.container > div {
  width: 40%;
  margin: 20px auto;
  text-align: center;
  /*
  To give the display a natural rounded shape, and to
```

```
 give it the appearance of
   "popping out", we have assigned a border radius and box
shadow CSS property
   */
   border-radius: 10px;
   box-shadow:0px 0px 3px -1px rgba(100,100,100,0.75);
}

/*
We choose some light colors as the background colors of
our displays
*/
.temperature{
   background-color: #ffcdd2
}

.humidity{
   background-color: #c5cae9
}

/*
We want our title to have a large size, and our value to
have the largest
size
*/
.container .title {
   font-size: 1.2em;
}

.container .value {
   font-size: 2em;
}

/*
We style our header so that it occupies the entire upper
band of the screen, and
also add a box-shadow so that we get a sense of it
popping out.
*/
header {
   text-align: center;
   font-size: 2em;
   padding: 15px;
   box-shadow:0px 3px 3px -1px rgba(0,0,0,0.75);
   background-color: #efebe9;
}
```

After adding CSS, open the app on your favorite browser:

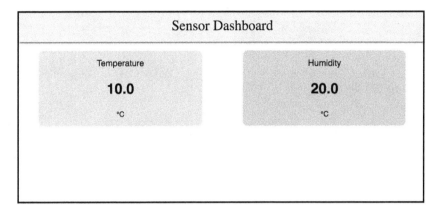

Your dashboard looks much more pleasant now.

Summary

This chapter was all about enhancing the quality of our user experience. We did not add anything as far as the underlying systems are concerned, but we greatly increased the value of our application to the end user. As we have seen, this can be done in three ways:

- **By adding a functionality to our frontend :** This is where we added the ability to call our APIs through scripts instead of navigating to the API directly. This gave us the base of our renewed experience because we were able to simultaneously call the temperature and humidity APIs from the same page.
- **By adding structure to our document:** Making a structured layout and placing the elements of our document accordingly gives us the ability to extend our UI further (as we will see in the next chapter).
- **By styling our layout:** This step seems like the most drastic change appearance-wise. If you showed before and after pictures of the website to a layman, they would most likely say the greatest change was in this section, and this is why it is so important to add CSS and style to your web application.

Our sensor dashboard now looks visibly cleaner and more appealing than it was in any of the previous chapters. We don't have to stop here, though. There are many more ways in which we can make our UI more intuitive and provide even more insight to our users. The next chapter will deal with more advanced visual elements to make our dashboard come alive.

Enhancing Our UI - Using Interactive Charts

An important thing to note during the development of any application is that the experience of the user is paramount. In the end, all we are really doing when we make applications is valuing our users' time. If we manage to save the user some effort in thinking or understanding some piece of data, we know we are moving in the right direction.

In the previous chapter, this is exactly what we were focusing on by combining the temperature and humidity readings into a single interface and, after that, by highlighting the relevant pieces of information through the modification of size and color by using CSS.

In this chapter, we will be continuing with the concept of user experience improvement by introducing advanced UI elements such as charts, which will help us interpret and understand the data even further.

Here's what we will be covering in this chapter:

- Introducing the the Chart.js library
- Building HTML5 charts using the Chart.js library
- Enhancing our server to provide consumable responses
- Injecting our sensor data into our chart

Considerations when implementing complex features

When it comes to building complex features in any software application, it often boils down to two options:

- Building each feature from scratch, thoroughly testing and integrating it into your application
- Using an existing library that has already taken care of the preceding point

Each option has its own trade-offs. If we decide to implement a feature and build it from scratch, we will have full control over what happens, and can customize it the way we like without any dependency. However, we must also take into consideration the time and effort that we will have to spend in building it. Even after spending months, there may still be scenarios and optimizations that we did not think of. These will, of course, be fixed as time passes, but this is time that could be spent elsewhere.

In contrast, we have numerous libraries available in the open source ecosystem at our disposal. Many smart people have spent time to develop code that we can reuse for our own purposes. In most mature libraries, this code has been battle tested and you can be certain that it takes care of almost all scenarios that may come up. The downside is that you have little control over the new features and bug fixes that get pushed from time to time. Furthermore, the library may not work exactly the way you want it to work for your application's use case.

The general rule of thumb when it comes to making this choice is this: if the feature you are trying to implement is relatively common, there is probably a library out there that does it better than you can.

With charts, which are one of the most common graphical elements in any data-driven dashboard, this is indeed the case.

Introducing Chart.js

Following up the discussion in the last section, choosing a library to create charts appears to be the most logical choice. There are a lot of popular libraries to choose from. Out of these, the most popular are as follows:

- **D3** (https://d3js.org/)
- **Chart.js** (http://www.chartjs.org/)

- **Highcharts** (`https://www.highcharts.com/`)

D3 is more of a general purpose library, and even though it's really great at making charts, there is still a lot of boilerplate code that has to be written to get a simple chart running.

Highcharts solves this problem by providing an easy configuration-based API that lets us create rich charts with just a few lines of code, but it comes with a very restricted license. This essentially means that any commercial applications are out of the question unless you get a paid subscription.

Chart.js gives us the best of both worlds. It provides us with an easy-to-use API to make rich, interactive charts and comes with an MIT license, which is very open and unrestrictive, both for personal as well as commercial use.

Installing Chart.js

You can get the latest version of the library here: `https://cdnjs.com/libraries/Chart.js`
.

As the time of writing this, the script to include in our HTML file is as follows:

```
<script src="https://cdnjs.cloudflare.com/
ajax/libs/Chart.js/2.6.0/Chart.bundle.js" >
</script>
```

Include this before you include your `script.js` file; otherwise, its code will not know that Chart.js exists.

To verify your installation, open your browser and inspect the `Chart` global variable in the browser's console. You should see that it is defined as the Chart.js constructor.

If you see this, it means that the installation of the Chart.js library is successful.

Creating our first chart

Before we integrate with our server, let's create a chart with dummy data to see how it works.

Chart.js works on the HTML canvas. The `canvas` element was included in the HTML5 standard, and it makes use of the GPU to render pictures and visual elements at an accelerated pace. This ultimately leads to a better experience when viewing the resultant charts, even with considerable amounts of data.

Let's start by placing our canvas elements in our dashboard. This is how our updated `index.html` file will look:

```
<!DOCTYPE html>
<html lang="en">

<head>
  <title></title>
  <meta charset="UTF-8">
  <meta name="viewport" content="width=device-width,
initial-scale=1">
  <!--The stylesheet is added here. We haven't made it
 yet, so don't worry if you get an error at this point-->
  <link href="style.css" rel="stylesheet">
</head>

<body>

  <header>Sensor Dashboard</header>

  <div class="container">

    <div class="temperature">
      <p class="title">Temperature</p>
      <p class="value" id="temperature-
display">Loading... </p>
      <p class="unit" >°C</p>
    </div>

    <div class="humidity">
      <p class="title">Humidity</p>
      <p class="value" id="humidity-display">Loading...
      </p>
      <p class="unit" >°C</p>
    </div>
  </div>
      <!--
```

```
   There's a new element with the container class. The
chart container will inherit the style of the previous
displays.
   -->
  <div class="container">
      <div>
        <!--
        The 100% width implies that we want the canvas
element to take the full width of its container, which
in this case remains the same width as the sensor values
display

        The height is fixed. Its generally good practice
to have relative widths and absolute heights in a
downward scrolling document
          -->
        <canvas id="temperature-chart" width="100%"
height="400px">
      </div>
      <div>
        <canvas id="humidity-chart" width="100%"
height="400px">
      </div>
  </div>

  <script
  src="https://cdnjs.cloudflare.com/ajax/libs/
  Chart.js/2.6.0/Chart.bundle.js" >
  </script>
  <script src="script.js"></script>
</body>

</html>
```

After this, the chart needs to be instantiated and drawn through JavaScript. Put this snippet anywhere in the existing `script.js` file:

```
/**
* Get the context of the temperature canvas element
*/
const temperatureCanvasCtx =
document.getElementById('temperature-
chart').getContext('2d')

/**
 * Create a new chart on the context we just instantiated
*/
const temperatureChart = new Chart(temperatureCanvasCtx,
```

```
{
  /**
   * Were going to show the ongoing temperature as a line
chart
   */
  type: 'line',
  data: {
    /**
     * This is mock data.
     * The labels, which will form our x-axis, are
 supposed to represent the time at which each reading was
 taken.
     * Finally, we add the dataset, whose data is an
 array of temperature values.
     * The background color is set to the same value as
 the earlier display, with some added transparency (which
 is why the 'rgba' representation is used)
     */
    labels: ['10:30', '10:31', '10:32', '10:33'],
    datasets: [{
      data: [12, 19, 23, 17],
      backgroundColor: 'rgba(255, 205, 210, 0.5)'
    }]
  },
  options: {
    /**
     * There is no need for a legend since there is only
 one dataset plotted
     * The 'responsive' and 'maintainAspectRatio' options
 are set so that the chart takes the width and height of
 the canvas, and does not set it on its own.
     */
    legend: {
      display: false
    },
    responsive: true,
    maintainAspectRatio: false
  }
})
```

Open your browser again to see the fully rendered chart. Hover over any of the points, and a tooltip with the readings' value should pop up:

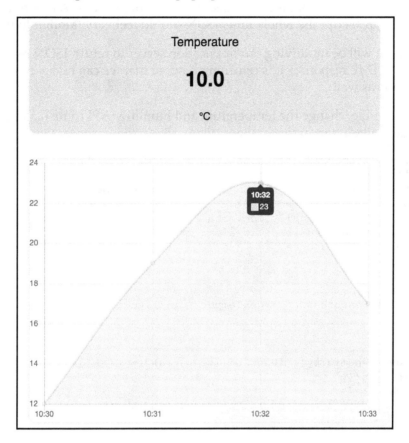

Making the server response data-friendly

Our server is currently returning HTML responses. A humidity of 38% will give us this response:

```
<strong>38</strong>
```

While this works for our current setup, it is not ideal for when we need raw data, like we do now for making our charts. It is far easier to convert raw data to HTML as opposed to doing the opposite, so we can make our sensor displays compatible for raw data as well.

The most popular standard for data interchange, and one that is almost universal now, is **JavaScript Object Notation** (JSON). JSON is a very simple data interchange specification that is used to serialize data that is exchanged between applications. As we have been programming in JavaScript the whole time, JSON should feel very familiar to us.

In this section, we will be modifying our application server to return JSON responses, as opposed to the HTML responses it is returning now, so that we can make use of the raw data in our charts as well.

In your `index.js` file, change the temperature and humidity API route handlers to the following code:

```
app.get('/temperature', function (req, res) {
  /**
   * The express response object comes with a built in
`json` method
   * This automatically converts its first argument into
a JSON string, and sends it along with the content type
headers as a response.
   */
  res.json({
    value:
getCachedSensorReadings.getTemperature().toFixed(1)
  })
})

app.get('/humidity', function (req, res) {
  res.json({
    value:
getCachedSensorReadings.getHumidity().toFixed(1)
  })
})
```

Modifying the sensor dashboards to consume JSON data

We must not forget that the sensor displays used earlier are currently set up to work with HTML text, not JSON data. In order to make it compatible, we will have to make a change to our script file. Fortunately, our code is made such that the only change to be made on our side is in the `fetchTemperature` and `fetchHumidity` functions:

```
const fetchTemperature = () => {
  fetch('/temperature')
    .then(results => {
```

```
    /**
     * We want the results converted to json, so we use
the fetch results' `json` method, which returns a promise
with the JSON data instead of the string
     */
    return results.json()
  })
  .then(data => {
    /**
     * In our server API route handler, the format of
returned data was an object with a `value` property.
     * The value of the sensor reading is therefore
available in `data.value`
     */
    const temperatureDisplay =
document.getElementById('temperature-display')
    /**
     * We add in the HTML tags on the front end script
this time, leaving the backend to only provide us data
     */
    temperatureDisplay.innerHTML = '<strong>' +
data.value + '</strong>'
  })
}
/**
 * Repeat the same steps for the humidity API
 */
const fetchHumidity = () => {
  fetch('/humidity')
    .then(results => {
      return results.json()
    })
    .then(data => {
      const humidityDisplay =
 document.getElementById('humidity-display')
      humidityDisplay.innerHTML = '<strong>' + data.value
+ '</strong>'
    })
}
```

If you open your browser, the app should look exactly the same as it did earlier, which is a good thing because that means we can move on to utilizing this data to power our charts.

Integrating sensor data into our charts

The goal of this section is to have our sensor data reflect in our charts. We know that readings are measured every two seconds. This means that we will also have to update our charts every two seconds. This is a slightly different situation when compared to the sample chart we created earlier because there are some assumptions that we didn't consider:

- The constant readings from the sensor require that our chart be dynamic. The values plotted have to change every time a new reading comes.
- We must choose a sensible scale. Our sample chart had values from 12 to 23. In the real world, temperature and humidity readings rarely change that often or that drastically, especially when we are measuring on a per-second timescale.

Fortunately, the Chart.js library has features to take care of both of these new findings. Let's modify our code to have a more sensible range for our temperature and humidity values and to dynamically inject readings as and when they are received.

First, we create a generic function, which accepts an array, a value, and a maximum length. Its job is to make sure we have a set of readings with a fixed length. If a new reading comes in, the oldest reading in this set is pushed out, such as a fixed length queue:

```
const pushData = (arr, value, maxLen) => {
  /*
  Push the new value into the array
  */
  arr.push(value)

  /*
  If the length of the array is greater than the maximum
  length allowed, push the first element out (through the
Array#shift method)
  */
  if (arr.length > maxLen) {
    arr.shift()
  }
}
```

 Remember, arrays and objects in JavaScript are passed by reference. So, any time we call this function with an array, that array is being directly modified by it.

Next, we change the chart configuration to take care of the range:

```
/*
Here, we take the configuration out and declare it as a
variable first.
*/
const temperatureChartConfig = {
  type: 'line',
  data: {
    /*
    For our actual data, we will not have any readings
initially
    */
    labels: [],
    datasets: [{
        data: [],
        backgroundColor: 'rgba(255, 205, 210, 0.5)'
    }]
  },
  options: {
    legend: {
      display: false
    },
    responsive: true,
    maintainAspectRatio: false,
    /*
    Add in the range for the Y-axis. Where I live, the
temperature varies from 15-35 °C
    With a 5 °C buffer range, that gives us a minimum
value of 10 and maximum of 40
    */
    scales: {
      yAxes: [{
        ticks: {
          suggestedMin: 10,
          suggestedMax: 40
        }
      }]
    }
  }
}
```

We are using the `suggestedMin` and `suggestedMax` properties in our Chart.js configuration. Like the naming suggests, these maximum and minimum values are only suggested and not hard fixed. What this means is that Chart.js will maintain this range, but if by some miracle the temperature goes above or below the suggested limits, the chart will change its minimum or maximum range values to fit the extreme values of our readings. This will happen rarely, if ever, but it's good to prepare for the outlier cases as well.

The `callback` code from the API call is now modified to inject every new sensor reading into the chart dataset:

```
const fetchTemperature = () => {
  fetch('/temperature')
    .then(results => {
      return results.json()
    })
    .then(data => {
      /*
      Note the time when the reading is obtained,
      and convert it to hh:mm:ss format
      */
      const now = new Date()
      const timeNow = now.getHours() + ':' +
now.getMinutes() + ':' + now.getSeconds()

      /*
      Add the data to the chart dataset

      The x-axis here is time, with the time of
measurement added as its value. Since it is measure in
regular intervals,
      we do not need to scale it, and can assume a
uniform regular interval
      The y-axis is temperature, which is stored in
`data.value`

      The data is being pushed directly into the
configuration we described above.
      A maximum length of 10 is maintained. Which means
that after 10 readings are filled in the dataset, the
older readings will start being pushed out.
      */
      pushData(temperatureChartConfig.data.labels,
  timeNow, 10)
      pushData(temperatureChartConfig.data.datasets[0]
  .data, data.value, 10)

      /*
```

```
`temperatureChart` is our ChartJs instance. The
`update` method looks for changes in the dataset and
axes, and animates and updates the chart accordingly.
    */
    temperatureChart.update()
    const temperatureDisplay =
document.getElementById('temperature-display')
    temperatureDisplay.innerHTML = '<strong>' +
 data.value + '</strong>'
    })
  }
```

The same logic is repeated for our humidity API.

A code overview

It looks like we've done a lot so far, so let's take a look at the overall uncommented code up until this point to get a better overview of what has been done so far.

The only files that were modified in this chapter were index.js, public/index.html, and public/script.js.

The final contents of these files is shown below:

index.js

```
const express = require('express')
const path = require('path')
const app = express()
const getCachedSensorReadings = require('./get-cached-
sensor-readings')

app.use('/public', express.static(path.join(__dirname,
 'public')))

app.get('/temperature', function (req, res) {
 res.json({
   value:
getCachedSensorReadings.getTemperature().toFixed(1)
 })
})

app.get('/humidity', function (req, res) {
  res.json({
    value: getCachedSensorReadings.getHumidity()
```

```
      .toFixed(1)
    })
})

app.listen(3000, function () {
  console.log('Server listening on port 3000')
})
```

public/index.html

```html
<!DOCTYPE html>
<html lang="en">

<head>
  <title></title>
  <meta charset="UTF-8">
  <meta name="viewport" content="width=device-width,
initial-scale=1">
  <link href="style.css" rel="stylesheet">
</head>

<body>

  <header>Sensor Dashboard</header>

  <div class="container">

    <div class="temperature">
      <p class="title">Temperature</p>
      <p class="value" id="temperature-
display">Loading... </p>
      <p class="unit">°C</p>
    </div>

    <div class="humidity">
      <p class="title">Humidity</p>
      <p class="value" id="humidity-display">Loading...
      </p>
      <p class="unit">°C</p>
    </div>

  </div>

  <div class="container">
    <div>
      <canvas id="temperature-chart" width="100%"
 height="400px">
```

```
    </div>
    <div>
      <canvas id="humidity-chart" width="100%"
height="400px">
      </div>
  </div>

  <script
src="https://cdnjs.cloudflare.com/ajax/libs/
Chart.js/2.6.0/Chart.bundle.js">

  </script>
  <script src="script.js"></script>
</body>

</html>
```

public/script.js

```
const temperatureCanvasCtx =
document.getElementById('temperature-
chart').getContext('2d')

const temperatureChartConfig = {
  type: 'line',
  data: {
    labels: [],
    datasets: [{
      data: [],
      backgroundColor: 'rgba(255, 205, 210, 0.5)'
    }]
  },
  options: {
    legend: {
      display: false
    },
    responsive: true,
    maintainAspectRatio: false,
    scales: {
      yAxes: [{
        ticks: {
          suggestedMin: 10,
          suggestedMax: 40
        }
      }]
    }
  }
}
```

```
}
const temperatureChart = new Chart(temperatureCanvasCtx,
temperatureChartConfig)

const humidityCanvasCtx =
document.getElementById('humidity-
chart').getContext('2d')

const humidityChartConfig = {
  type: 'line',
  data: {
    labels: [],
    datasets: [{
      data: [],
      backgroundColor: 'rgba(197, 202, 233, 0.5)'
    }]
  },
  options: {
    legend: {
      display: false
    },
    responsive: true,
    maintainAspectRatio: false,
    scales: {
      yAxes: [{
        ticks: {
          suggestedMin: 30,
          suggestedMax: 90
        }
      }]
    }
  }
}
const humidityChart = new Chart(humidityCanvasCtx,
 humidityChartConfig)

const pushData = (arr, value, maxLen) => {
  arr.push(value)
  if (arr.length > maxLen) {
    arr.shift()
  }
}

const humidityDisplay =
document.getElementById('humidity-display')
const temperatureDisplay =
document.getElementById('temperature-display')
```

```
const fetchTemperature = () => {
  fetch('/temperature')
    .then(results => {
      return results.json()
    })
    .then(data => {
      const now = new Date()
      const timeNow = now.getHours() + ':' +
 now.getMinutes() + ':' + now.getSeconds()
      pushData(temperatureChartConfig.data.labels,
timeNow, 10)
      pushData(temperatureChartConfig.data.datasets[0]
.data, data.value, 10)
      temperatureChart.update()
      temperatureDisplay.innerHTML = '<strong>' +
data.value + '</strong>'
    })
}

const fetchHumidity = () => {
  fetch('/humidity')
    .then(results => {
      return results.json()
    })
    .then(data => {
      const now = new Date()
      const timeNow = now.getHours() + ':' +
now.getMinutes() + ':' + now.getSeconds()
      pushData(humidityChartConfig.data.labels, timeNow,
 10)
      pushData(humidityChartConfig.data.datasets[0].data,
 data.value, 10)
      humidityChart.update()
      humidityDisplay.innerHTML = '<strong>' + data.value
 + '</strong>'
    })
}

setInterval(() => {
  fetchTemperature()
  fetchHumidity()
}, 2000)
```

If these files look good to you, run the `index.js` file using the node and open your browser to see a fully functional dashboard with dynamic animated charts:

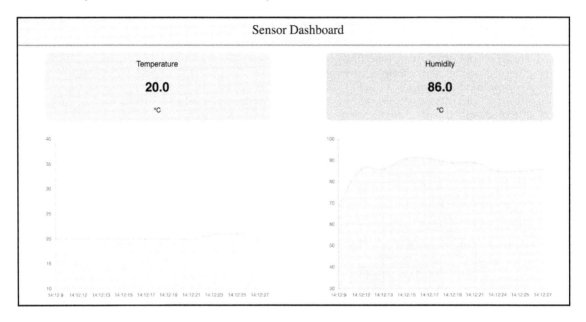

Summary

Throughout this chapter, we modified almost all aspects of our code in order to make it more data friendly.

First, you learned the basics of the Chart.js library. We also reasoned about why we are choosing Chart.js over other similar libraries. We went on to make a sample chart using this library, to be used in the later part of the chapter to integrate with out sensor readings.

To prepare for this, the server was made more data friendly through the use of JSON responses. Our frontend was then optimized to utilize these responses.

We finally made use of Chart.js' ranging and data animation features to make our charts look more to scale and to make them dynamic with respect to displaying new data.

Our frontend now looks much richer and more like a fully featured dashboard. However, there are still a few features that we are missing. If you notice, every time we refresh our web page, the data that was there on the chart disappears.

Take a moment to think about why this happens and what you would do to solve it. In the next section, we will address this problem and you will learn how to make our data more persistent.

8

SQLite - The Fast and Portable Database

We concluded the previous chapter with a problem, which was that none of our data was really there. All the temperature and humidity readings we took using our sensor were rather ephemeral and disappeared as soon as we closed our browser.

Overall, there is great value in storing our data:

- It leads to a better experience for the user because, if they refresh or close their browser, the information that they were looking at will still be there.
- It gives us access to information that we could not obtain earlier. How does the temperature today compare to the temperature of yesterday for the same time of the day? How about last week?
- It gives us a chance to implement new features for our application, such as filtering readings based on the time of the day or searching and sorting through the readings for a given time period.

In this section of the book, we will be covering topics on how to make our data persistent through the use of simple-to-use open source tools.

We will cover the following topics:

- Picking the correct tool for the job
- Creating the temperature and humidity tables
- Running CRUD operations
- Aggregations
- About SQLite and its architecture

- SQLite installation on the Pi
- Creating a database and executing queries in SQLite

Picking the correct tool for the job

Similar to what we did in the previous chapter, let's look at why we choose the tools that we use. Our requirements for choosing a database are as follows:

- The solution should be portable
- Ease of installation and learning--we want to get up and running as fast as possible
- Compatible with the Raspberry Pi
- Lightweight since we are running it on our Pi with limited resources
- Feature-rich enough to support the requirements of our application

SQLite is one such database that fits these requirements quite well:

- **Portability**: SQLite can be run almost anywhere, with minimal dependencies. The only thing that SQLite relies on to maintain all your data is a single file on your system. What this means when you want to transfer your entire database to another machine is that the only thing you have to give them is the database file that your SQLite instance was using.
- **Lightweight and ease of use**: SQLite does not have any other dependencies, unlike most other databases. Just ask anyone who has ever installed MySQL. There is a single binary, which you run while specifying which file to use and get going.
- **Standards compliant**: SQLite uses the SQL database query language and consequently comes along with its rich features. It's like getting all the features of modern feature-rich relational databases with none of the overhead of configuration and set up.

Of course, there is no such thing as a silver bullet. SQLite has all these great features as a trade-off for other commonly used features:

- **No user management**: There is no provision for managing users and their rights to different databases. SQLite cannot be used with a multi-user application where access to each database must be fine-tuned.
- **Limited write operations**: SQLite allows only one write operation to take place at any time, so anything related to concurrency gets thrown out of the window.

The application we are building, however, is not affected by any of these limitations because:

- There is only one user, that is, our server application. All the regular users of our application do not directly access our database; they only do it through the server.
- We do not have high volume write operations. The purpose of having persistent storage is that we can record the readings as and when they are captured. This happens once every 2 seconds, and so we do not have to think about high volumes in this case.

For these reasons, the SQLite database is the best-suited choice for our use case.

Installation

To install SQLite on the Pi, run the command:

```
sudo apt-get update
sudo apt-get install sqlite3
```

To verify the installation, run this:

```
sqlite3 -version
```

If all went well, this command should print the current version of sqlite installed.

Starting a an SQLite database is as simple as running the following:

```
sqlite3
```

This will open the sqlite3 shell:

```
SQLite version 3.19.3 2017-06-08 14:26:16
Enter ".help" for usage hints.
Connected to a transient in-memory database.
Use ".open FILENAME" to reopen on a persistent database.
sqlite>
```

You are now in a fully functional SQL shell and can execute most of the SQL commands that you are familiar with if you have used other SQL-based databases. When you run SQLite 3 like this, it runs an in-memory database without storing it permanently (as hinted in the opening logs of the shell).

To run the database with persistent storage, provide an argument to the `sqlite3` command, indicating the location of the file that you want SQLite to use in order to store data:

```
sqlite3 ~/.sqlite.db
```

From this point on, this is the command you can use to start the SQLite database, and `.sqlite.db` is the file that we direct SQLite to use in order to store its data.

Creating the temperature and humidity tables

For our application, we will be creating two tables, one each for our temperature and humidity readings. The structure will be similar for both of them:

- The `createdAt` column to store the date and time of creation
- The `value` column to store the actual value read by the sensor

When creating the table, it's useful to know SQLites datatypes. This will not be a hard task since there are only five:

- TEXT
- NUMERIC
- INTEGER
- REAL
- BLOB

In most other relational databases, there is a data type for `datetime`, which we would have used for our `createdAt` column. In the case of SQLite, the `datetime` is represented either as a string in the ISO format (YYYY-MM-DD HH:MM:SS), or as an integer in Unix time (the time elapsed since 1970-01-01 00:00:00 UTC).

From this, we decide the types of these:

- `createdAt` as TEXT (ISO formatted `datetime`)
- `value` as REAL

Start up the SQLite shell and enter these commands to create your temperature and humidity tables:

```
CREATE TABLE temperature (createdAt TEXT, value REAL);
CREATE TABLE humidity (createdAt TEXT, value REAL);
```

To see the list of all tables available, run the following command:

.tables

This would give you an output of :

```
sqlite> .tables
humidity        temperature
```

There are a few important reasons why two tables for temperature and humidity were chosen instead of just one table with the `createdA`, `temperatureValue`, and `humidityValue` columns:

- Even though the single table model represents the way by which we receive readings now (currently, we obtain both temperature and humidity readings at the same time, so the `createdAt` value would be identical for them) , that may not be the same in the future. If you have noticed, we have separated the functionality for temperature and humidity in all the other chapters including this one because this way, we can also handle cases where the readings are taken separately, through different sensors.
- We make room for more readings in the future. If we are required to measure another quantity in the future (such as the intensity of light or atmospheric pressure), we can just add more tables and extend the functionality for the rest of the application, just like we did for temperature or humidity. If we used a single table for everything, it would be difficult to add new columns in the future due to the difference in time of measurement and all the NULL values we would have to account for in the time when they didn't exist.

Running CRUD operations

CRUD is short for **Create**, **Read**, **Update**, **Delete**, which are the four essential operations that are run on any database.

Now that we have created tables to hold our temperature and humidity readings, let's run some basic operations on them to get the hang of SQLite and the SQL syntax.

For the purpose of this chapter, only the temperature table will be used, but the commands can be easily translated to be used on the humidity table as well.

Create

We start by inserting a dummy value into our temperature table:

```
INSERT INTO temperature VALUES (datetime('now'), 16.7);
```

This is standard SQL syntax, where we direct SQLite to insert the current datetime and dummy value of 16.7 into our temperature table. The order of values should be the same as the order of columns defined in our CREATE TABLE statement from before.

The datetime function is specific to SQLite. Based on its arguments, it returns the datetime in a number of formats. When we call this function with the argument of now, it returns the current date and time at the moment of calling the datetime function in the ISO string format (for example, 2017-06-18 12:13:50).

Read

The SELECT command is used to read data from our database. Start by just printing all the data in the temperature table (currently, one row):

```
SELECT * FROM temperature;
```

This will give you an output of this:

```
2017-06-18 12:13:50|16.7
```

Your createdAt value will differ based on when you ran the INSERT statement.

The values of each row are separated by the | character.

Run a few more dummy inserts so that we can see the filtering capabilities of SQLite:

```
INSERT INTO temperature VALUES (datetime('now'), 16.9);
INSERT INTO temperature VALUES (datetime('now', '+1
second'), 14.7);
INSERT INTO temperature VALUES (datetime('now', '+2
second'), 22);
INSERT INTO temperature VALUES (datetime('now', '+3
second'), 21.1);
```

Your temperature table should now look similar to this:

createdAt	Value
2017-06-18 12:13:50	16.7
2017-06-18 12:26:08	16.9
2017-06-18 12:26:09	14.7
2017-06-18 12:26:10	22.0
2017-06-18 12:26:13	21.1

Using SQL, you can filter the rows and columns that you want to pick from your data.

To filter columns, you explicitly mention the one you want to pick instead of the wildcard (*):

```
SELECT "value" from temperature;
```

This statement prints only the `value` column from our temperature table:

```
16.7
16.9
14.7
22.0
21.1
```

To filter rows, use the `WHERE` directive along with the filter condition:

```
SELECT * FROM temperature WHERE createdAt > "2017-06-18
12:26:09";
```

With this statement, only the rows where the `createdAt` date is after `2017-06-19 10:52:50` are displayed:

```
2017-06-18 12:26:10|22.0
2017-06-18 12:26:13|21.1
```

We can combine both of these types of filters as well:

```
SELECT "value" FROM temperature WHERE createdAt > "2017-
06-18 12:26:09";
```

This will display all values from the temperature table whose readings were taken after `2017-06-19 10:52:50`:

```
22.0
21.1
```

As you can probably tell, filters are going to be a very important application in fetching the correct data for us, and we are going to deal with them quite a lot going forward.

Update

The `UPDATE` statement is used to change or modify existing database records. The format is as follows:

```
UPDATE <table name> SET <colum name>=<new value> WHERE
  <filter condition>;
```

As an example, if there was some sensor error and we found out that the reading we took at `2017-06-18 12:26:08` was actually `16.6`, we would have the following:

- Table name: `temperature`
- Column name: `value`
- New value: `16.6`
- Filter condition: `createdAt = "2017-06-18 12:26:08"`

So, our resulting SQL statement would be as follows:

```
UPDATE temperature SET value=16.6 WHERE createdAt="2017-
06-18 12:26:08";
```

The filter condition after the `WHERE` directive is the same as any filter we may put while reading. If there are multiple records matching the filter, they will all be updated.

Delete

To delete records, the `DELETE` statement is used. Its format is similar to the update statement without any values to set, of course:

```
DELETE FROM <table name> WHERE <filter condition>;
```

If we wanted to make room for new records by deleting all records older than `2017-06-18 12:26:08`, we would have the following:

- Table name: `temperature`
- Filter condition: `createdAt < "2017-06-18 12:26:08"`

This would result in the following:

```
DELETE FROM temperature WHERE createdAt < "2017-06-18 12:26:08";
```

The resultant table after the update and delete statements is as follows:

createdAt	value
2017-06-18 12:26:08	16.6
2017-06-18 12:26:09	14.7
2017-06-18 12:26:10	22.0
2017-06-18 12:26:13	21.1

Aggregations

The power of SQL and SQLite does not end just in simple CRUD operations. SQLite exposes a number of useful functions that can be utilized to obtain even more meaningful insights from your data.

Some of the functions that we will be using to enhance our application are as follows:

- `avg(X)`: Returns the average of all values passed to it
- `max(X)`: Returns the maximum value out of the values passed to it
- `min(X)`: Returns the minimum value out of the values passed to it
- `count(X)`: Returns the total number of values passed to it

Here, X denotes the column name to be aggregated.

 Most of the functions provided by SQLite work on both text as well as numeric input. For example, max and min would also work on text input by ordering the provided values alphabetically. However, some functions (such as avg) may not make sense for text inputs, and although they return a result, they are mostly unusable.

To find the average temperature, run this:

```
SELECT avg(value) FROM temperature;
```

This will return the single value of "18.6".

Similarly, run a command for the maximum value:

```
SELECT max(value) FROM temperature;
```

This will return "22.0".

As with any other read query, filters can be used. So, if we only wanted to find the maximum temperature that was read before "2017-06-18 12:26:10", we could run the following:

```
SELECT max(value) FROM temperature WHERE createdAt <
  "2017-06-18 12:26:10";
```

We would receive "16.6" as the output.

Advanced aggregations using subqueries

The result of all our aggregations was a single value. This single value can also be used as a scalar to perform operations on more advanced queries. These scalars are used in the form of subqueries.

A subquery is a query within a query, in simple terms. The result of one query is used to obtain the result of another query.

For example, the result obtained from the averaging query can be used to selectively print only those temperatures that were above average:

```
SELECT * FROM temperature
WHERE value > (SELECT avg(value) FROM temperature);
```

 Queries can be multi-line as well.

In the preceding query, `(SELECT avg(value) FROM temperature)` is executed first, and the value obtained from it (since it is one-dimensional) is used to specify the filter for the higher-level query. This query will give us the following result:

createdAt	value
2017-06-18 12:26:10	22.0
2017-06-18 12:26:13	21.1

In addition to filtering, we can also use subqueries to modify the displayed results of a normal query. To illustrate this, consider the following query, which gives us the deviation of each temperature from the average, in addition to the information we already receive:

```
SELECT value,
(SELECT avg(value) FROM temperature) - value,
createdAt
FROM temperature;
```

In the second line, we direct the query to give us an additional column, which is the difference in the average (whose value is evaluated from the subquery) and the value of the temperature in each row. We then get the resulting table:

value	deviation	createdAt
16.6	2.0	2017-06-18 12:26:08
14.7	3.9	2017-06-18 12:26:09
22.0	-3.4	2017-06-18 12:26:10
21.1	-2.5	2017-06-18 12:26:13

The power of SQLite seems more apparent now since we just displayed information that wasn't even present in our table.

Summary

SQL is a very powerful language, and SQLite brings us all this power in a lightweight, easy-to-install, and open source software.

Initially, we went through the reasons why we chose SQLite as our database solution and why it's a good choice for our particular use case. In the process, we also went over some of the strengths and weaknesses of SQLite.

You then learned how to set up a running SQLite instance on our Pi. After that, we understood the data types used by SQLite and decided the schema for our data tables. We used this to initialize some tables to hold the data of our application.

After this, we discovered some basic CRUD operations to read and write selectively to our database using the SQL language. Finally, we took our queries to the next level by learning some advanced queries that used aggregations and subqueries.

This chapter was important as a base for the next chapter, which is where we will learn to integrate the knowledge we obtained on database management that you learned in this chapter with our existing server application.

9
Integrating SQLite into Our Application

In the previous chapter, we took a look at SQLite and the functionality it can provide us in order to persist our data. We ended up learning a lot about SQLite but did not make any change to our existing application. In this chapter, we are going to get back down to our application core and enhance it to support data persistence with SQLite!

Integrating SQLite into our application requires some consideration to the following topics:

- How to interface our running SQLite instance with node.
- When to update the database with our data.
- When to read from the database. We will make use of our existing caching module to make this more efficient.

We also discussed the numerous possibilities that adding persistence was going to enable. We can't just let that go to waste. In this chapter, we will also be adding new features, such as the following:

- Fetching historical results so that the charts don't go blank on each refresh.
- Adding the ability to view temperature from a particular date range and display the average temperature in that date range.

Specifically, we will cover the following topics:

- Interfacing SQLite with node
- Running queries with node
- Making our database module

- Integrating the database module into our server
- Adding new features - the ability to view readings from a custom time period

Getting started: Interfacing SQLite with node

Before we add any new features, we first have to get node and SQLite to play nice with each other.

Fortunately, there is a library to make our lives easier (`https://www.npmjs.com/package/sqlite3`). The way this package works is interesting enough for it to be worth mentioning. The node module itself comes with a running SQLite instance, which interfaces with the file containing all your data. This is in contrast to other database interfaces, which connect to a running database instance.

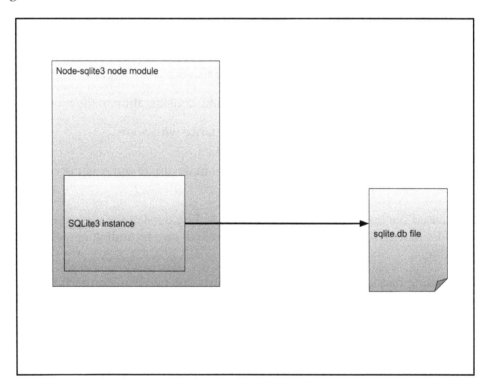

Running queries with node

In the previous chapter, we executed all our queries in a file called `.sqlite.db`. We will use this same file to demonstrate how to execute queries and receive their results inside our node process:

```
/**
 * Import the SQLite library, and initialize the SQLite db
instance
 * Mention the location of the ".sqlite.db" file that you
used in the previous chapter
 * We want the absolute path of the file, for better
   clarity, hence, the use of path.resolve
 * The location inside path.resolve, is the location of the
   sqlite.db file relative to this one
 */
const sqlite3 = require('sqlite3')
const path = require('path')
const db = new
    sqlite3.Database(path.resolve('././sqlite.db'))

/**
   * The "serialize" method of the db instance makes sure
     that all queries directly in its callback are executed
   sequentially
   */
db.serialize(function () {
  /**
     * db.run is used to execute write queries (UPDATE,
   CREATE and DELETE).
     * Since this is called inside the "serialize" callback,
   it will be executed in series, and a callback is not
   required.
     */
  db.run('UPDATE temperature SET value=21.3 WHERE
   createdAt="2017-06-24 10:27:25"')
  /**
     * The "all" method of the db instance means that we want
   to return all results matching the given query, and returns
   it in the "results" argument in the callback function
     */
  db.all('SELECT * FROM temperature', (err, results) => {
    if (err) {
      console.error(err)
    }
    console.log(results)
  })
```

```
})

/**
 * At this point, we are done with the database. Close the
connection after the queries execute
 */
db.close()
```

In the preceding code snippet, you learned how to run both `read` and `write` queries on our database. Next, let's make a module that specializes in running the database operations for us.

Making our database module

Currently, our application requires the following features with respect to data persistence:

- Adding a new temperature to the database when it is recorded.
- Fetching historical temperature results so that our charts don't go blank. This can be rephrased as fetching the past 10 temperature results to initially populate our chart.
- Fetching temperatures for a particular date range.
- Fetching the average of temperatures in a date range.

In order to implement these features, we need to create a new module. In this module, each of the four points listed is implemented as separate methods of the singleton returned by the module.

Adding a new temperature to the database

In order to insert a value into one of our tables, we need only two pieces of information:

- The value
- The type of reading taken (whether temperature or humidity)

Let's construct a function that takes these two as parameters and performs the insert operation:

```
const insertReading = (type, reading) => {
  db.run(`INSERT INTO ${type} VALUES (datetime('now'),
${reading});`)
}
```

The date and time of the reading are handled by SQLite's datetime function.

The query is generated with ES6 template strings.

Fetching the last "n" readings from a table

For this operation, we need the following:

- The type of reading desired
- The number of readings we want

```
const fetchLatestReadings = (type, limit, callback) => {
  db.all(`SELECT * FROM ${type} ORDER BY createdAt DESC
 LIMIT ${limit}`, callback)
}
```

Since we want the readings returned from the query, we use the all method to return all readings. Furthermore, since this operation is asynchronous, a callback needs to be supplied. Since this function is being exported, the callback is provided as an argument to the function and passed on to the db.all method.

Fetching readings between a certain time period

For this operation, we need the following:

- The type of reading desired
- The two times between which we require readings

```
    const fetchReadingsBetweenTime = (type, start,
end,
    callback) => {
     db.all(`SELECT * FROM ${type} WHERE createdAt
  > ? AND
     createdAt < ?;`, [start, end], callback)
    }
```

In this query, we do not use template string variables and go for the library's query parameterization instead. Query parameterization is when we use a query template and fill it in with the required values, as opposed to hardcoding the entire query. The reason we do this is to prevent SQL injection. In all our previous queries, we were constructing the query within our system. These queries were not going to be exposed outside our server application.

This query is different in the sense that we plan to let the user choose the times between which they would like to see readings. The `start` and `end` parameters are, therefore, susceptible to outside interference and must be provided as query parameters to prevent SQL injection.

> You can go to `https://www.sohamkamani.com/blog/2016/11/24/what-is-sql-injection/` to learn more about SQL injection.

Fetching the average of readings between time periods

This is similar to the previous query in terms of the information we require in order to obtain the average:

```
const getAverageOfReadingsBetweenTime = (type, start, end,
    callback) => {
  db.get(`SELECT avg(value) FROM temperature WHERE
createdAt > ? AND createdAt < ?;`, [start, end], callback)
}
```

In this function, we're using the `get` method instead of the `all` method since we expect only one reading to be returned.

Putting the functions together in a module

To create a module, place all the preceding functions in a single file and export them so that they can be used by other parts of our application:

```
/*
We have to first instantiate the "db" database instance
before using it in our functions
*/
```

```
const sqlite3 = require('sqlite3')
const path = require('path')
const db = new
sqlite3.Database(path.resolve('./.sqlite.db'))

const insertReading = (type, reading) => {
  db.run(`INSERT INTO ${type} VALUES (datetime('now'),
    ${reading});`)
}

const fetchLatestReadings = (type, limit, callback) => {
  db.all(`SELECT * FROM temperature ORDER BY createdAt
DESC LIMIT ${limit}`, callback)
}

const fetchReadingsBetweenTime = (type, start, end,
 callback) => {
  db.all(`SELECT * FROM temperature WHERE createdAt > ?
AND createdAt < ?;`, [start, end], callback)
}

const getAverageOfReadingsBetweenTime = (type, start, end,
callback) => {
  db.get(`SELECT avg(value) FROM temperature WHERE
createdAt > ? AND createdAt < ?;`, [start, end], callback)
}

/*
Export all the functions we just created as methods to the
exported singleton
*/
module.exports = {
  insertReading,
  fetchLatestReadings,
  fetchReadingsBetweenTime,
  getAverageOfReadingsBetweenTime
}
```

Save this file as `database-operations.js` in the same folder as our other modules.

As a reference, our folder structure now looks like this:

```
.
├── database-operations.js
├── get-cached-sensor-readings.js
├── get-sensor-readings.js
├── index.js
├── package.json
```

```
└── public
    ├── index.html
    ├── script.js
    └── style.css
```

Integrating the database module into our server application

Now that we have our database module ready, it's time to use the functionality we just created and update our existing modules to make use of this persistence.

Upgrading the sensor interface module

The functionality defined in `get-cached-sensor-readings.js` was defined to fetch readings from our sensor and return it via a `callback` function. Now that we have our database in place, we want to store the readings in addition to returning them:

```
const getSensorReadings = require('./get-sensor-readings')

/**
 * Import the database module that we created earlier
 */
const databaseOperations = require('./database-
operations')

const cache = {
  temperature: 0,
  humidity: 0
}

setInterval(() => {
  getSensorReadings((err, temperature, humidity) => {
    if (err) {
      return console.error(err)
    }
    /**
     * In addition to storing the readings in our cache,
we also store them in our database, using the methods
that we exported from our module
     */
    databaseOperations.insertReading('temperature',
temperature)
```

```
            databaseOperations.insertReading('humidity', humidity)
            cache.temperature = temperature
            cache.humidity = humidity
        })
    }, 2000)

    module.exports.getTemperature = () => cache.temperature
    module.exports.getHumidity = () => cache.humidity
```

One question that may arise is this: Why are we implementing this in `get-cached-sensor-readings.js` and not `get-sensor-readings.js`?

As we have also seen in the previous chapters, one of our aims is to make the system as flexible as possible. The responsibility of the `get-sensor-readings.js` file was to interface with the external sensor and return the readings. The responsibility of `get-cached-sensor-readings.js` is to get readings and store them. Since storing readings in our database closely matches this responsibility, it makes sense to bundle the functionality here.

Furthermore, if we decided to change the sensor interface one day, we would also have to modify the code that was stored our readings. In the current situation, the code to interface with the sensor can change as long as the abstraction it provides is consistent.

Adding an API to get the latest ten readings

We want the frontend of our application to get the last ten readings to populate the initial values of the chart. To do this, we're going to add another API to get the readings from the database:

```
    app.get('/temperature/history', function (req, res) {
        databaseOperations.fetchLatestReadings('temperature', 10, (err,
    results) =>
        {
            if (err) {
                /**
                 * If any error occured, send a 500 status to the frontend and
    log it
                 */
                console.error(err)
                return res.status(500).end()
            }
            /**
             * Return the reverse of the results obtained from the database.
             */
            res.json(results.reverse())
```

```
    })
  })
```

An interesting thing to note is that we do not return the results as we get them from the database. Instead, we return the reversed results. This is because the charts accept data in ascending order, whereas we obtain them from the database in descending order due to the limit we put in the query.

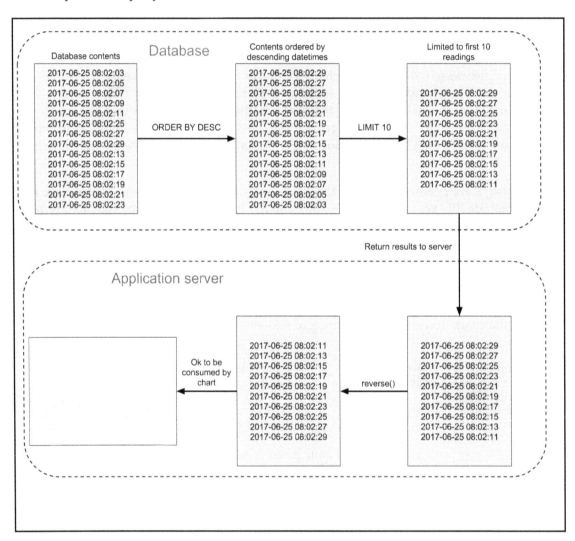

Consuming the API on the client side

Now that we have an API to fetch the last ten readings, we have to consume it on the client side. We add the following code to the `public/script.j` file:

```
const fetchTemperatureHistory = () => {
  /**
   * Call the APi we created
   */
  fetch('/temperature/history')
    .then(results => {
      return results.json()
    })
    .then(data => {
      data.forEach(reading => {
        /**
         * For each reading present in the "data" array,
         * convert the time to the ISO Z format accepted
 by the javascript Date object
         * Format the time and push data on to the chart,
  similar to the previous API calls
         */
        const time = new Date(reading.createdAt + 'Z')
        const formattedTime =
        time.getHours() + ':' + time.getMinutes() + ':' +
 time.getSeconds()
        pushData(temperatureChartConfig.data.labels,
formattedTime, 10)
        pushData(temperatureChartConfig.data.datasets[0]
.data, reading.value, 10)
      })

      /**
       * Finally, update the chart after all readings have
  been pushed
       */
      temperatureChart.update()
    })
}

fetchTemperatureHistory()
```

Similarly, we can add the functionality for humidity.

For the API, this is the code:

```
app.get('/humidity/history', function (req, res) {
  databaseOperations.fetchLatestReadings('humidity', 10,
(err, results) => {
    if (err) {
      console.error(err)
      return res.status(500).end()
    }
    res.json(results.reverse())
  })
})
```

And, for the client side, this is the code:

```
const fetchHumidityHistory = () => {
  fetch('/humidity/history')
    .then(results => {
      return results.json()
    })
    .then(data => {
      data.forEach(reading => {
        const time = new Date(reading.createdAt + 'Z')
        const formattedTime =
        time.getHours() + ':' + time.getMinutes() + ':' +
  time.getSeconds()
        pushData(humidityChartConfig.data.labels,
      formattedTime, 10)
        pushData(humidityChartConfig.data.datasets[0].data,
    reading.value, 10)
      })
      humidityChart.update()
    })
}

fetchHumidityHistory()
```

Restart your app and view it in the browser now. Every time you refresh the page, the chart readings stay. Furthermore, if you close your browser and open the app after some time, it will show you the latest 10 readings from the time before your opened your application. We just added persistence to our application. Awesome!

Adding new features - the ability to view readings from a custom time period

Adding persistence gives us a very small end result even though there is a lot going on under the hood. Now is the best time to make use of the power we have with SQLite to add more features to our application.

Adding the required APIs

Just like in the previous section, we will need to start by adding the APIs to get the readings and their average for a certain time period:

```
app.get('/temperature/range', function (req, res) {
  /**
   * Here, the "start" and "end" datetimes for the range
 of readings are
   * expected to be received through the query parameters.
 This is spllied as part
   * of the URL request
   */
  const {start, end} = req.query

  /**
   * The "fetchReadingsBetweenTime" method is called,
 which returns an array of results, which we return as
 JSON to the client side
   */
  databaseOperations.fetchReadingsBetweenTime
('temperature', start, end, (err, results) => {
    if (err) {
      console.error(err)
      return res.status(500).end()
    }
    res.json(results)
  })
})

app.get('/temperature/average', function (req, res) {
  const {start, end} = req.query
  databaseOperations.getAverageOfReadingsBetweenTime
('temperature', start, end, (err, results) => {
    if (err) {
      console.error(err)
      return res.status(500).end()
```

```
    }
    /**
     * This is similar to the earlier API, except that we
   just return a singular value.
     * The signature is therefore more reminisent of the
   "/temperature" API
     */
    res.json({
      value: results['avg(value)'].toFixed(1)
    })
  })
})
```

Next, we add the required client-side code to the `public/script.js` file:

```
/**
 * We first define a function to extract the parameters
 from the request query.
 * You do not need to be concerned too much with its
implementation, although you could always study it as an
excercise.
 */
function getParameterByName (name) {
  const url = window.location.href
  name = name.replace(/[\[\]]/g, '\\$&')
  const regex = new RegExp('[?&]' + name +
    '(=([^&#]*)|&|#|$)')
   const results = regex.exec(url)
  if (!results) return null
  if (!results[2]) return ''
  return decodeURIComponent(results[2].replace(/\+/g, '
  '))
}

const fetchTemperatureRange = () => {
  /**
   * The getParameterByName function is used to get the
   "start" and "end"
   * parameters from the query
   */
  const start = getParameterByName('start')
  const end = getParameterByName('end')

  /**
   * These parameters are then passed on to make AJAX
  requests to get the range of
   * readings from the server
   */
```

```
    fetch(`/temperature/range?start=${start}&end=${end}`)
      .then(results => {
       return results.json()
     })
      .then(data => {
       data.forEach(reading => {
         /**
          * These readings are pushed to the chart
          */
         const time = new Date(reading.createdAt + 'Z')
         const formattedTime =
           time.getHours() + ':' + time.getMinutes() + ':'
 + time.getSeconds()
          pushData(temperatureChartConfig.data.labels,
formattedTime, 10)
         pushData(
            temperatureChartConfig.data.datasets[0].data,
           reading.value,
            10
         )
       })
       temperatureChart.update()
     })
   /**
     * We also use this information to fetch the average by
calling the required
     * API, and updating the reading display with the result
     */
   fetch(`/temperature/average?start=${start}&end=${end}`)
     .then(results => {
      return results.json()
     })
     .then(data => {
        temperatureDisplay.innerHTML = '<strong>' +
data.value + '</strong>'
     })
 }
```

We similarly create the APIs for humidity and the fetchHumidityRange function on the client side.

There is one step left. If the user wishes to view a range of readings, we should not update the chart with new readings, like we did earlier. Conversely, there is no need to fetch the range if the user wishes to see the live readings. To handle these cases, we add this snippet of code at the end of the file:

```
if (!getParameterByName('start') &&
!getParameterByName('end')) {
  /**
   * The fetchTemperature and fetchHumidity calls are now
moved here
    * and are called only when the "start" and "end"
 parametes are not present in the query
   * In this case, we will be showing the live reading
 implementation
   */
  setInterval(() => {
    fetchTemperature()
    fetchHumidity()
  }, 2000)
  fetchHumidityHistory()
  fetchTemperatureHistory()
} else {
  /**
   * If we do have these parameters, we will only be
showing the range of readings requested by calling the
functions we defined in this section
   */
  fetchHumidityRange()
  fetchTemperatureRange()
}
```

All that's left now is to see our app in action! To view a range of readings, go to a URL similar to the following:

```
http://localhost:3000/public/?start=<start
 datetime>&end=<end datetime>
```

Replace the `start` and `end` parameters with a URL encoded version of your datetime string (for example, `http://localhost:3000/public/?start=2017-06-25 08:44:16&end=2017-06-25 08:45:00`)

Now your browser should display all readings in this range without a live update:

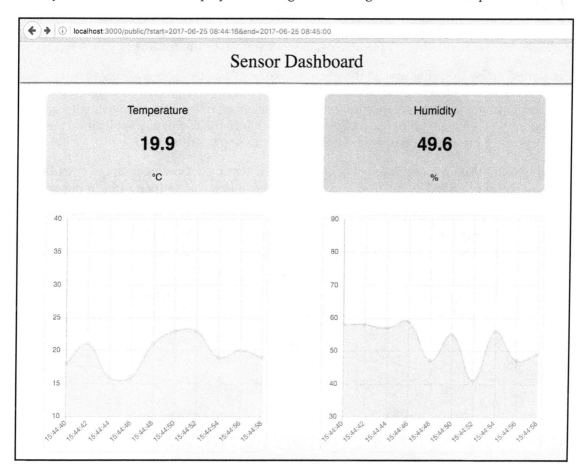

To go back to live readings, simply remove the query from the URL (go to `http://localhost:3000/public/` again)

Summary

With this chapter, we finally gave our application a memory ability greater than that of a goldfish, and we finally have a place to permanently store all the readings that we record.

We started off by studying how to interface SQLite3 using node. This was core to our application since all the other application code would depend on it. After we figured out the basics, we managed to create a module that specialized in reading and writing to our database. We then went on to use this module to enhance the rest of our application and finally remove the annoying phenomenon of disappearing charts.

Finally, we moved on to adding two completely new features: showing a range of readings between dates provided by the user and showing the average of temperatures in this range.

It looks like we have covered all the parts of the web application stack that we discussed in Chapter 1, *Getting Started on the Raspberry Pi* and made quite a lot of progress in implementing features in our application. However, there are still more features of the modern web that we can make use of.

In the next chapter, you will learn about an alternate method of obtaining readings from the server, through web sockets: something that will make our application truly real-time.

10
Making our Application Real Time with Web Sockets

If you thought our application was real time until now, you would be wrong. Currently, our application gives us the appearance of being instant, but in reality, this is just the browser polling the server for information every once in a while (in our case, once in a while meant two seconds in the previous chapters).

While you may be thinking that this is okay since there is rarely any actual need to know the temperature or humidity with an urgency greater than a few seconds, there is still another problem that we haven't considered, and that is the large amount of useless data that is passed around because of this method of getting information. In a majority of cases, the temperature or humidity is stable (as far as our desired accuracy of a single decimal point is concerned) for much longer than a few seconds and changes only once every few minutes. This means that a lot of the AJAX calls that we make to our server just tell us that our readings haven't changed.

One of the solutions to this problem is to just increase the waiting time between API calls so that it is more reflective of the actual average time period between which readings change. However, if we do this, we do it at the cost of being instantaneous. Suddenly, we are faced with the choice of being perfectly instantaneous and perfectly efficient with our data but not both.

Fortunately for us, there is still a way in which we could solve this problem: what if the server could notify the client when there were any changes instead of the client constantly asking the server after every fixed time interval? This is exactly what we hope to achieve with the help of web sockets and, consequently, make our application truly real-time.

In this chapter, we will cover the following topics:

- Web sockets
- Implementing web sockets in our application
- Creating our socket implementation in our application server
- Client-side implementation

Web sockets

Web sockets run on top of the web socket protocol, which is a TCP protocol that provides a framework for two-way communication between the client and the server.

This is different from the standard request reply model, in which only the client can initiate a request to the server and only then, receive a response.

Web sockets work by first establishing a socket connection. This is actually done by initiating an HTTP request, so technically, it is still the client that initiates the request for a socket connection, and only after that request is fulfilled and a connection is established can the server send over information independently to the client:

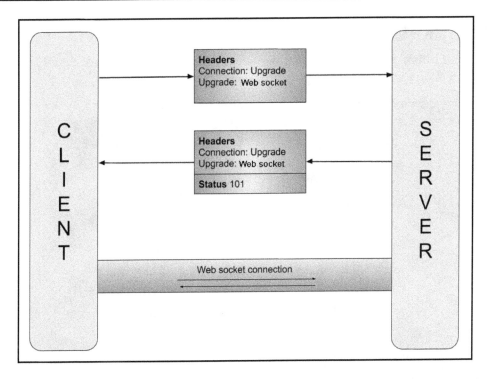

The request to initiate a web socket connection comes with special headers (**Connection** and **Upgrade**) that indicate that the client wishes to switch to the web socket protocol.

The server (if it supports web sockets) then responds with corresponding headers and a **101** (switching protocol) status, along with some additional headers for security. Once this is done, the client and server can successfully communicate using the web socket protocol.

Implementing web sockets in our application

If all this talk of the web socket protocol and its functioning sounded complex, that's because it is. We could make this entire implementation ourselves and spend a few days or even weeks on it, but as with previous chapters, the boring stuff is already taken care of by an external library called `socket.io` `https://socket.io/`.

`Socket.io` provides both client-side and server-side libraries and abstracts away most of the complicated stuff, such as establishing a connection and pushing information, and abstracts it behind a convenient API for developers to use.

The socket.io library

The `socket.io` library provides a convenient abstraction to the process of establishing a socket connection as well as sending and receiving messages.

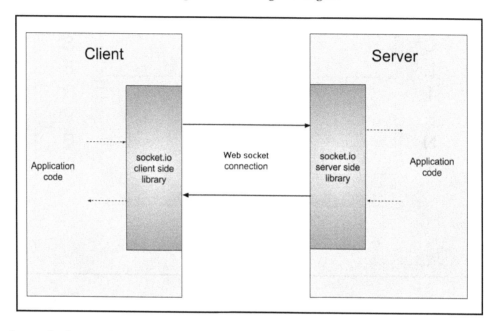

It works on the basis of event emitters and event listeners. Both the client as well as the server can emit or listen to events.

Event listeners or emitters can be declared on a socket instance. This socket instance is created on the browser and the server every time a new connection is established. The client will have a single instance for itself, and the server will have multiple instances for each client connected to it.

If we want to emit an event, we use the `emit` method of our socket instance:

```
socket.emit('event-name', data)
```

On the other hand, we can declare a listener to a socket event:

```
socket.on('event-name', data => {
  /*
  Do something with the data that was emitted
  */
})
```

Because there are multiple clients that can connect and disconnect from the servers socket connection, we need to put handlers in place for these events. For this library, these are the **"connection"** and **"disconnect"** events. The overall flow can be summed up like this:

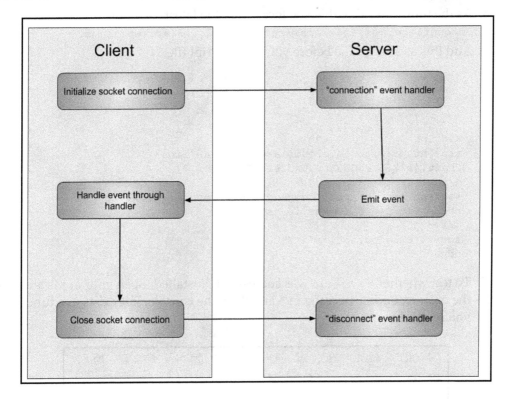

Client-side installation

The `socket.io` provides a client-side library to abstract the browser side socket connection establishment and communication. First, we need to install this library so that we can use it in our client-side code:

1. To add `socket.io` to our client-side script, we have to include the external script file provided by `socket.io`.
2. To view the location and latest versions of the required script files, you can visit this page: `https://cdnjs.com/libraries/socket.io`.
3. As the time of writing this, the location of the latest script file is at `https://cdnjs.cloudflare.com/ajax/libs/socket.io/2.0.3/socket.io.js`.
4. Add this as a script file before your main script file:

   ```
   ...
   ...
   ...

     <script
     src="https://cdnjs.cloudflare.com/ajax/libs/
     Chart.js/2.6.0/Chart.bundle.js">
     </script>
     <script src="https://cdnjs.cloudflare.com/ajax/libs/
     socket.io/2.0.3/socket.io.js">
     </script>
    <script src="script.js"></script>
   </body>
   ```

5. To test whether `socket.io` was successfully installed, open your application in the browser and inspect the `io` variable in the console. If it exists as a function, you're good to go:

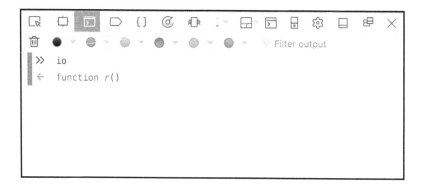

Server-side installation

`Socket.io` also provides its server-side implementation through its `socket.io` node module. To install it, run the command:

```
npm install --save socket.io
```

You can now use the `socket.io` library by `require` it in the application code, which we will be looking at in the next section.

Creating our socket implementation in our application server

Before we begin, let's recap the features that we want to implement:

- The server should notify the client
- Notifications should be pushed only if the reading changes

The first requirement means that we have to replace our `/temperature` and `/humidity` API calls with their socket notification equivalents. The second requirement means that we need a way to link our implementation of the first requirement with a mechanism to only push notifications when a reading changes:

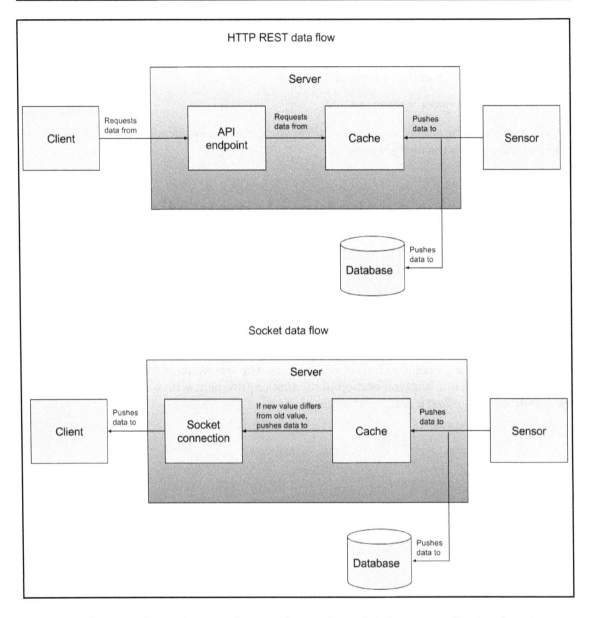

It is generally a good practice to make sure that each module in our application functions independently and has only one job that it does well. Following this, it would be unwise to have our cache module communicate with the socket connection directly since:

- It is not either of their jobs to do so.

- This would cause problems in the future if we had to notify the socket connection for something else. We would have to reimplement communication with whatever other modules we wished to be notified by.

To solve this, we would need to create another module for the sending and receiving of event notifications. This module would have functions to subscribe to an event (to be used in the socket connection definition) and to push notifications to them (to be used by the cache) `notifier.js`:

```
/**
 * Define the listeners (for temperature and humidity)
 */
const listeners = {
  temperature: [],
  humidity: []
}

/**
 * The subscribe function takes two arguments, the
 callback function, and the type.
 * It pushes the provided listener to our array of
 listeners (either the temperature listener array, or the
 humidity listener array, depending on the "type"
 provided)
 */
const subscribe = (listener, type) => {
  listeners[type].push(listener)
}

/**
 * If we wish to remove a listener from our list, we call
    the unsubscribe function.
 * This accepts the exact same types of arguments as the
 subscribe function
 */
const unsubscribe = (removedListener, type) => {
  /**
   * The list of listeners is sifted through and the
  listener functions are filtered on
   * the basis of whether they are the same as the
  listener provided
   * Those that are the same (which would be only one)
  are removed
   */
  listeners[type] = listeners[type].filter(listener =>
listener !== removedListener)
```

```
}

/**
 * The notify function is used by the cache when it
 receives an update from the sensor
 * It takes a value and a type as an argument, and
 notifies all the listeners of that type that a new value
 has been received
 */
const notify = (value, type) => {
  listeners[type].forEach(listener => {
    listener(value)
  })
}

/**
 * The functions that are to be used by other modules are
 exported
 */
module.exports = {
  subscribe, unsubscribe, notify
}
```

Now that the backbone of the communication system is in place, let's make use of it in our other modules. First, the cache module is modified so that in addition to updating the cache values and executing database operations, it also notifies everyone who is listening for changes to the temperature and humidity sensor readings get-cached-sensor-readings.js.:

```
const getSensorReadings = require('./get-sensor-
  readings')
const databaseOperations = require('./database-
  operations')
 /**
  * Import the notify function from the notifier module
  */
 const {notify} = require('./notifier')

const cache = {
  temperature: 0,
  humidity: 0
}

setInterval(() => {
  getSensorReadings((err, temperature, humidity) => {
    if (err) {
      return console.error(err)
```

```
      }
    databaseOperations.insertReading('temperature',
temperature)
    databaseOperations.insertReading('humidity',
humidity)

    /**
     * Check whether the incoming values from the sensor
   are the same as the previous values (that were stored in
   cache)
     * If they are different, notify all listers of the
   given type
     */
    if (cache.temperature !== temperature) {
      notify(temperature, 'temperature')
    }
    if (cache.humidity !== humidity) {
      notify(humidity, 'humidity')
    }
    cache.temperature = temperature
    cache.humidity = humidity
  })
}, 2000)

module.exports.getTemperature = () => cache.temperature
module.exports.getHumidity = () => cache.humidity
```

Finally, add the following code snippet to the `index.js` file:

```
/**
 * Import the external dependencies required, for us this
is:
 * 1. The native http module
 * 2. The socket.io module that we installed
 * 3. The subscribe and unsubscribe functions from the
notifier module
 */
const http = require('http')
const socketIo = require('socket.io')
const {subscribe, unsubscribe} = require('./notifier')

/**
 * Create a new HTTP server that wraps the "app" object
 that defined our server
 */
const httpServer = http.Server(app)

/**
```

```
 * Socket.io implements its own routes on top of the
existing ones by wrapping our HTTP server
 */
const io = socketIo(httpServer)

io.on('connection', socket => {
  /**
   * This callback is called every time a new client
successfully makes a websocket connection with our server
   */
  console.log(`User connected [${socket.id}]`)

  /**
   * The event listeners are defined inside the callback
function because we need to access the "socket" instance,
to emit changes to the client
   * The "pushTemperature" and "pushHumidity" listeners
are called on change of temperature and humidity
respectively.
   */
  const pushTemperature = newTemperature => {
    socket.emit('new-temperature', {
      value: newTemperature
    })
  }

  const pushHumidity = newHumidity => {
    socket.emit('new-humidity', {
      value: newHumidity
    })
  }

  /**
   * Subscribe the listeners that we just defined to the
"temperature" and "humidity" events
   */
  subscribe(pushTemperature, 'temperature')

  subscribe(pushHumidity, 'humidity')

  socket.on('disconnect', () => {
    /**
     * Finally, when the connection is closed,
unsubscribe the listeners from their events
     */
    unsubscribe(pushTemperature, 'temperature')
    unsubscribe(pushHumidity, 'humidity')
  })
```

```
})

/**
 * The httpsServer.listen method is called. This exposes
the routes we defined for the "app" instance as well
 */
httpServer.listen(3000, function () {
  console.log('Server listening on port 3000')
})

/**
 * The app.listen method invocation from the previous
version is removed, in place of the httpServer.listen
method
 */
// app.listen(3000, function () {
//   console.log('Server listening on port 3000')
// })
```

Client-side implementation

Now that the server side is completed, the client-side script needs to be modified to accommodate the new functionality that has been added:

```
/**
 * First, define a function that will initialize the
socket connection and add listeners
 * to the required events
 */
const addSocketListeners = () => {
  /**
   * The "io" constructor is available to us after
including the socket.io library script in the     "index.html" file
   * Initializing the socket connection is as easy as the
statement below
   */
  const socket = io()

  /**
   * An event listener is attached to the "new-
temperature" event
 * The handler is similar to the handler that was attached
 to the GET /temperature API, so in essence, we are
replacing the API call with the socket event notification
   */
  socket.on('new-temperature', data => {
```

```
    const now = new Date()
    const timeNow =
  now.getHours() + ':' + now.getMinutes() + ':' +     now.getSeconds()
    pushData(temperatureChartConfig.data.labels, timeNow,
10)
    pushData(temperatureChartConfig.data.datasets[0].data,
data.value, 10)

    temperatureChart.update()
    temperatureDisplay.innerHTML = '<strong>' +
 data.value + '</strong>'
  })

  /**
   * Similarly, we add the handler for the "new-humidity"
event
   */
  socket.on('new-humidity', data => {
    const now = new Date()
    const timeNow =
  now.getHours() + ':' + now.getMinutes() + ':' +
 now.getSeconds()
    pushData(humidityChartConfig.data.labels, timeNow,
10)
    pushData(humidityChartConfig.data.datasets[0].data,
data.value, 10)

    humidityChart.update()
    humidityDisplay.innerHTML = '<strong>' + data.value +
'</strong>'
  })
}
if (!getParameterByName('start') &&     !getParameterByName('end')) {
  /**
   * Finally, the fetchHumidity and fetchTemperature
functions, that used to call the APIs at regular     intervals, are
removed.
   * In their place, the addSocketListeners function is
 called (and only needs to be called once this time)
   */
  addSocketListeners()

  // setInterval(() => {
    // fetchTemperature()
    // fetchHumidity()
  // }, 2000)
  fetchHumidityHistory()
  fetchTemperatureHistory()
```

```
    } else {
      fetchHumidityRange()
      fetchTemperatureRange()
    }
  }
```

Once this is done, open your browser, and you should see a subtle but significant change: the charts and dashboard values update only once the value of a reading has changed. Furthermore, the temperature and humidity charts now update independently and only if their own individual values change. This is because the client is only notified if the server detects a change in temperature or humidity. This might not look like much visually, but it is a huge change under the hood, which can be observed by looking at the network tab in your browser's inspector:

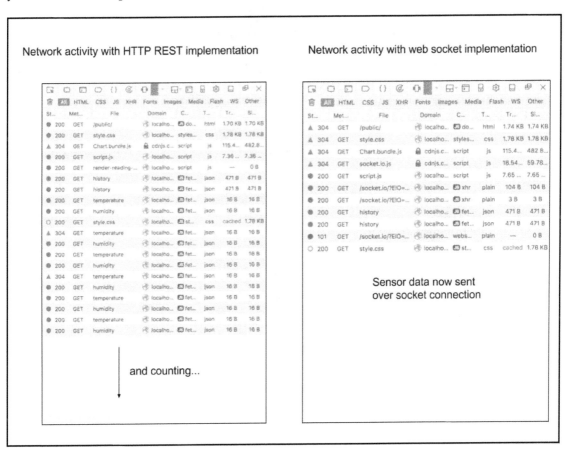

Summary

We started out this chapter by looking at the current problems facing our application. Following this, we looked at how web sockets can solve our problem and found a fully featured implementation of web sockets in the `socket.io` library. The basics of `socket.io` were covered in addition to how it was going to work with the current application. We then went on to actually implementing the `socket.io` library in both the client-side as well as the server-side application code and finally inspected the network activity in both cases to observe the difference.

Although web sockets seem like a solution to all our problems, there are still some drawbacks that we should consider:

- Web sockets are more resource-intensive compared to HTTP calls since each connection to the server is maintained as a separate instance and exists for as long as the client is active. HTTP calls, on the other hand, conclude when a response is sent by the server.
- While web sockets may work on almost all modern browsers, its support is still lacking in older browsers such as IE9 and Opera Mini.

Overall, web sockets should be utilized depending on the use case and considering the trade-offs involved.

Up until this point, everything we have worked on has been running on the Pi. In the next chapters, we will take off and break away from the confines of our Pi's hardware and move a lot of the functionality in our application to the cloud!

11
Deploying our application to Firebase

Everything we did up to this point was restricted to the confines of the Raspberry Pi hardware. Although the Pi is a marvel of engineering in and of itself, it still comes with some limitations due to its small size. While hosting small-scale personal applications should not be much cause for concern, it would not be efficient to host a large-scale application entirely on the Pi.

In addition to this, letting others access your application would be another challenge altogether. How does one ensure that their Pi is always online when people need it? How can we take the load of multiple users without compromising our hardware? How can we ensure that the connectivity from the Pi (which is running in our home) is seamless to someone trying to access it potentially across the world?

The answer to all these questions is that it is nearly impossible for a single portable computer sitting on someone's personal internet connection to overcome the challenges of scale. In order to do this, we would have to leverage the power of the cloud. It's much easier than you think, and there are a large number of paid and free solutions meant for exactly these problems, out of which Firebase is one of the most prominent.

In this chapter, we will go through the Firebase platform and explore the various tools that Firebase provides that can help solve some of the problems mentioned earlier.

Here's a brief overview of topics covered in this chapter:

- The Firebase platform
- Migrating our application to Firebase
- Creating a Firebase application

- Initializing Firebase Realtime Database
- Modifying the client-side code to accommodate the Firebase API

The Firebase platform

Getting full-scale applications up and running fast and bug-free is surprisingly hard. First, you have to provision your server, then your database, then your UI, and then you've to make sure all components integrate with each other correctly (which is the hardest part). This gets even harder when you want to introduce more advanced functionality, such as authentication, notifications, real-time updates, and encryption.

The Firebase platform solves this pain point by giving us all this out of the box:

- The **Realtime Database** is a tool to store and manage an applications persistent data as well as notify us when anything changes.
- Firebase hosting allows us to move all our frontend static assets to the cloud so that they can be delivered to users across the globe with speed and security.
- Performance monitoring and analytics give us in-depth information about our users and their interaction with our application.
- Firebase provides much more than this, which is outside the scope of our application, such as cloud lambda functions (serverless code execution), authentication, cloud storage APIs, and even notifications for mobile apps.

Migrating to Firebase

We covered the overall architecture of our application in the second chapter of this book. In order to migrate to Firebase, we need to rethink this architecture and see what we can leverage from the Firebase platform and, more importantly, what we can't.

The User interface

This is probably the easiest to decide. Our user interface takes the form of static files that need to be served to the user.

With Firebase Hosting, we can offload the task of serving static assets and files (arguably the highest load in terms of network traffic) entirely to the cloud.

Moreover, the reliability that a cloud solution provides will lead to faster and more secure retrieval of our static assets.

Database

Another major area that is resource-intensive is the database layer. We need a readily available server with enough storage space.

The Firebase Realtime database gives us a convenient way to access and store our data. It is a JSON storage engine, which means that it is schemaless. One of the most compelling features of the Realtime Database is that it gives us the ability to listen to and act on changes to our data. Essentially, this can completely replace the APIs that we previously created to fetch our data.

Server application and sensor interface

The sensor interface requires the server application to obtain readings from it periodically. Since physical objects are the only thing we cannot actually convert into software, this will have to stay on-premise.

We could move the application server to the cloud and use Firebase's cloud lambda functions to execute the same code that is currently being executed on the Pi, but then we would need to create another server on our Pi that exists just to fetch and server information from our sensor.

Since the core functionality of our application server is precisely this, it does not make sense to move the server to the cloud. In short, we need some kind of server on the Pi to fetch and send data.

We can, however, transform the server into a process and remove the APIs since we will no longer be needing them. Our APIs, then, which were previously used to retrieve the data on database, will move to the APIs that the Firebase Realtime Database provides out of the box

In the end, our modified architecture will utilize the best of both worlds:

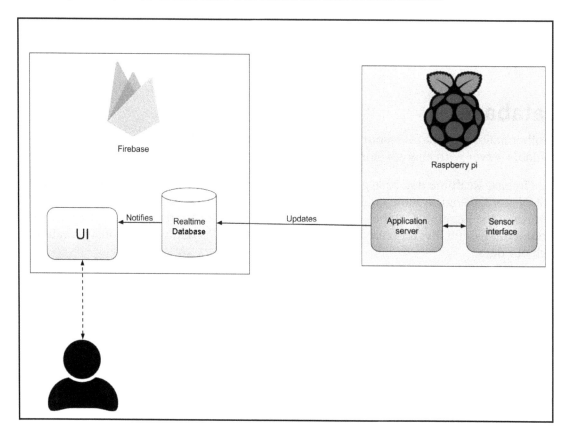

Creating your first Firebase application

To get started with Firebase, you will need to sign up and log in using their website: `https`
`://firebase.google.com/.`

Go to the Firebase console (by clicking on **GO TO CONSOLE**), and then click on the **Add project** button:

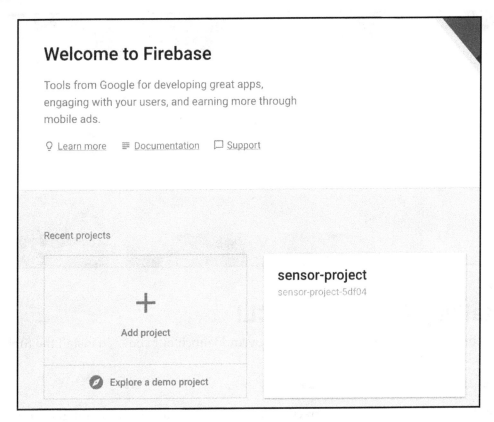

You will then be asked some details, after which your new project should be created (and show up in this panel, such as the **sensor-project** project that is already created)

You can explore your project's console and take a look at the various features and add-ons that Firebase provides:

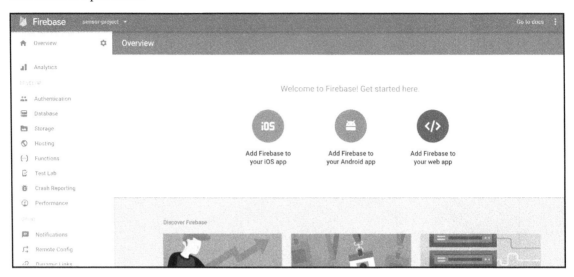

Installing the Firebase CLI

The Firebase CLI tools help us actually deploy and launch our code. To install the firebase CLI, run the command:

```
npm install -g firebase-tools
```

To test that it has been installed correctly, run this command, which should give you the version number of the installed files:

```
firebase --version
```

Logging in to Firebase on the command line

In order to use the CLI tools, you will have to log in and authorize the use of the Firebase CLI. Run the command:

```
firebase login
```

This will take you to a browser window and authenticate with your Google account. Once you authorize Firebase CLI, you will get a confirmation popup:

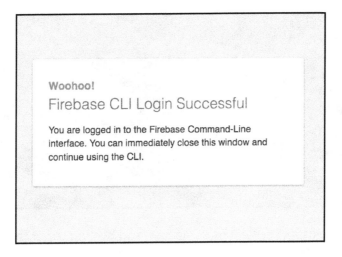

And then you will get a corresponding message on the Terminal.

Initializing a new Firebase application

Since the structure of a Firebase application is governed by convention, and since we are going to modify most of our code, let's gain a fresh start and create a new empty folder for our Firebase application. You can name it whatever you want... for the purpose of reference, I have named the folder `firebase`.

Navigate to this folder on the Terminal and run the command:

```
firebase init
```

This will open up an interactive tool and ask you a few questions, the first of which requires you to mention the services that will be used along with our application:

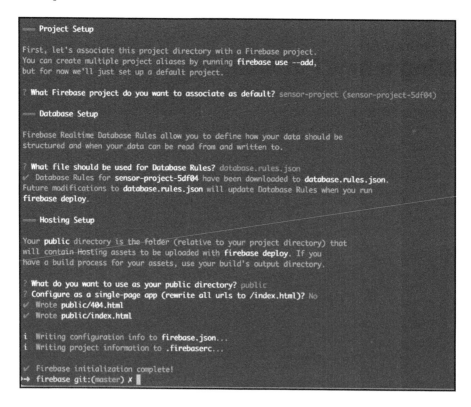

Currently, we will be using the Realtime Database and hosting. After this, a few more options will be presented:

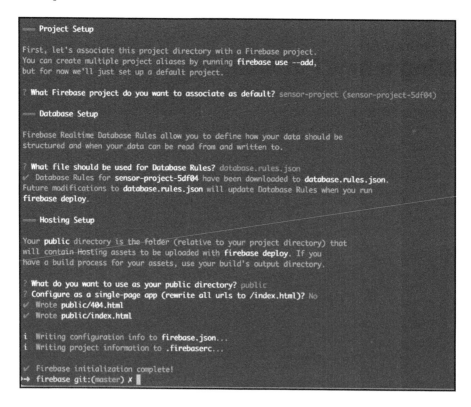

Choose the name of the application you just created on the Firebase console and select the default options for the configuration file locations.

After this, Firebase will create a bunch of files and folders:

```
.
├── database.rules.json
├── firebase.json
└── public
    ├── 404.html
    └── index.html
```

Following are the files and the folders:

- `firebase.json`: This is the central configuration file for the Firebase application, and it contains its common rules and file locations
- `database.rules.json`: This contains rules for the Realtime Database and its authorization
- `public`: This is the directory inside which all our static assets will live. Currently, it is filled with the default assets that Firebase has provided, which we will change later

Testing and deploying the application to the cloud

Now that we have a default application in place, run the command:

```
firebase serve
```

This will start and run a server on your local machine. The default port is 5000, so pointing your browser to `http://localhost:5000` should show you this page:

If you see this, then that means that Firebase is running correctly.

Next, we will deploy this application to the cloud. Run the command:

```
firebase deploy
```

This seemingly simple command uploads our entire Firebase application to the cloud within a matter of seconds!

```
▸→ firebase git:(master) ✗ firebase deploy

=== Deploying to 'sensor-project-5df04'...

i  deploying database, hosting
✔  database: rules ready to deploy.
i  hosting: preparing public directory for upload...
✔  hosting: public folder uploaded successfully
✔  hosting: 2 files uploaded successfully
i  starting release process (may take several minutes)...

✔  Deploy complete!

Project Console: https://console.firebase.google.com/project/sensor-project-5df04/overview
Hosting URL: https://sensor-project-5df04.firebaseapp.com
```

Navigate to the link presented at the end of deployment, and you should see your application running live on the Firebase platform.

Awesome! Now it's time to run *our* application the same way.

Migrating the frontend assets

The first part of moving to firebase is migrating our client-side files, which includes all of the HTML, CSS, and client-side JavaScript files we were serving earlier.

Our files are not going to be served on our application server anymore, and we will not be using its APIs anymore. In order to clean things up, we are going to remove the contents of all our API-invoking functions that were there in the client-side script, such as fetchTemperature, fetchHumidity, fetchHumidityHistory, fetchTemperatureHistory, fetchHumidityRange, and fetchTemperatureRange.

The resultant script.js file will look like this:

```javascript
const temperatureCanvasCtx = document
    .getElementById('temperature-chart')
    .getContext('2d')

const temperatureChartConfig = {
  type: 'line',
  data: {
    labels: [],
    datasets: [
      {
        data: [],
        backgroundColor: 'rgba(255, 205, 210, 0.5)'
      }
    ]
  },
  options: {
    legend: {
      display: false
    },
    responsive: true,
    maintainAspectRatio: false,
    scales: {
      yAxes: [
        {
          ticks: {
            suggestedMin: 10,
            suggestedMax: 40
          }
        }
      ]
    }
  }
}
const temperatureChart = new Chart(temperatureCanvasCtx,
```

```
temperatureChartConfig)

    const humidityCanvasCtx = document
      .getElementById('humidity-chart')
      .getContext('2d')

    const humidityChartConfig = {
      type: 'line',
      data: {
        labels: [],
        datasets: [
          {
            data: [],
            backgroundColor: 'rgba(197, 202, 233, 0.5)'
          }
        ]
      },
      options: {
        legend: {
          display: false
        },
        responsive: true,
        maintainAspectRatio: false,
        scales: {
          yAxes: [
            {
              ticks: {
                suggestedMin: 30,
                suggestedMax: 90
              }
            }
          ]
        }
      }
    }
    const humidityChart = new Chart(humidityCanvasCtx,
humidityChartConfig)

    const pushData = (arr, value, maxLen) => {
      arr.push(value)
      if (arr.length > maxLen) {
        arr.shift()
      }
    }

    const humidityDisplay =
     document.getElementById('humidity-display')
    const temperatureDisplay =     document.getElementById('temperature-
```

```
display')

    const fetchTemperature = () => {

    }

    const fetchHumidity = () => {

    }

    const fetchTemperatureHistory = () => {

    }

    const fetchHumidityHistory = () => {

    }

    /**
     * We first define a function to extract the parameters
    from the request query.
     * You do not need to be concerned too much with its
    implementation, although you could always study it as an     exercise.
     */
    function getParameterByName (name) {
      const url = window.location.href
      name = name.replace(/[\[\]]/g, '\\$&')
      const regex = new RegExp('[?&]' + name + '(=
([^&#]*)|&|#|$)')
      const results = regex.exec(url)
      if (!results) return null
      if (!results[2]) return ''
      return decodeURIComponent(results[2].replace(/\+/g, '
 '))
    }

    const fetchTemperatureRange = () => {

    }

    const fetchHumidityRange = () => {

    }

    if (!getParameterByName('start') &&     !getParameterByName('end')) {
      /**
       * The fetchTemperature and fetchHumidity calls are now
    moved here
```

```
    * and are called only when the "start" and "end"
  parametes are not present in the query
    * In this case, we will be showing the live reading
implementation
    */
  setInterval(() => {
    fetchTemperature()
    fetchHumidity()
  }, 2000)
  fetchHumidityHistory()
  fetchTemperatureHistory()
} else {
/**
  * If we do have these parameters, we will only be
  showing the range of readings requested by calling the        functions
we defined in this section
  */
  fetchHumidityRange()
  fetchTemperatureRange()
}
```

Now, these functions will not do anything, and as a result, our application will be a blank shell like it was earlier:

Since the `index.html` and `style.css` files do not involve any backend API calls, we can leave them be.

Copy all the front end files to the `public` directory inside your Firebase project. The directory structure will now resemble this:

```
.
├── database.rules.json
├── firebase.json
└── public
    ├── 404.html
    ├── index.html
    ├── script.js
    └── style.css
```

Adding Firebase tools

On the Firebase console home page (shown previously), click on **Add Firebase to your web app**.

You should see a popup that will give you the scripts that you then have to include in the `index.html` file:

Add these scripts to the `index.html` file just before the `script` tag that includes the `script.js` file:

```
    ...
    ...
    </div>

    <script      src="https://cdnjs.cloudflare.com/ajax/libs/Chart.js/2.6.
    0/Chart.bundle.js">

    </script>
    <script      src="https://www.gstatic.com/firebasejs/4.1.3/firebase.js
    "></script>
    <script>
      // Initialize Firebase
      var config = {
        apiKey: "......",
        authDomain: "sensor-project-5df04.firebaseapp.com",
        databaseURL: "https://sensor-project-
    5df04.firebaseio.com",
        projectId: "sensor-project-5df04",
        storageBucket: "sensor-project-5df04.appspot.com",
        messagingSenderId: "......"
      };
      firebase.initializeApp(config);

    </script>
    <script src="script.js"></script>
</body>
    ...
    ...
```

Adding the Realtime Database

To establish the connection with our Realtime Database, let's create a database and add some dummy data to it first.

Go to the **Database** tab in the Firebase console, and you should find a database with your application name.

Use the in-app editor to add dummy values for a `temperature` and `humidity` key:

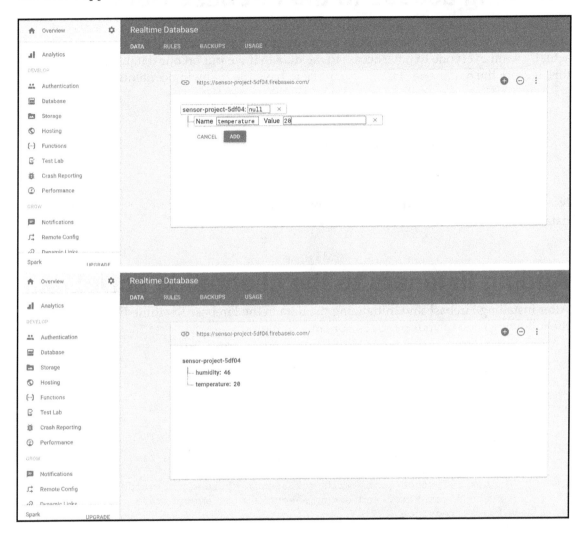

Now that we've added the database, let's connect to it from the frontend of our application.

Enabling access to the Firebase Database

Firebase provides us with a lot of security features. By default, an unknown user is not allowed to access data in the database from any frontend application. For our use case, we actually want everyone to have access to the data that we put on our database. To enable this, modify the `database.rules.json` file to have the following contents :

```
{
  "rules": {
      ".read": "auth == null",
      ".write": "auth != null"
  }
}
```

Now, everyone can `read` our data, and anyone who is authorized can `write` to our database.

Adding listeners to the client-side script

After installing Firebase and initializing the data in the Firebase Realtime Database, append the following code to your `public/script.js` file:

```
/**
 * Initialize a new database with the firebase.database
constructor
 */
const database = firebase.database()

/**
 * database.ref returns a reference to a key in the
realtime database.
 * This reference comes with a listener to read the value
for the first time, and execute some action everytime a
value is received
 */
const temperatureListener = database.ref('temperature')

temperatureListener.on('value', data => {
  /**
   * The contents of the listener are pretty much the
  same as the listeners in our previous chapters. The only
difference being that the value
   * of the data being read has to be accessed through      the "val"
getter method,
   * rather than the data.value attribute
```

```
    */
    const now = new Date()
    const timeNow =
    now.getHours() + ':' + now.getMinutes() + ':' +
now.getSeconds()
      pushData(temperatureChartConfig.data.labels, timeNow,      10)
      pushData(temperatureChartConfig.data.datasets[0].data,
data.val(), 10)
      temperatureChart.update()
      temperatureDisplay.innerHTML = '<strong>' + data.val()
    + '</strong>'
    })

    /**
     * Similarly, we add the corresponding references and       listeners for
    humidity
     */
    const humidityListener = database.ref('humidity')

    humidityListener.on('value', data => {
      const now = new Date()
      const timeNow =
      now.getHours() + ':' + now.getMinutes() + ':' +      now.getSeconds()
      pushData(humidityChartConfig.data.labels, timeNow, 10)
      pushData(humidityChartConfig.data.datasets[0].data,      data.val(),
10)
      humidityChart.update()
      humidityDisplay.innerHTML = '<strong>' + data.val() +      '</strong>'
    })
```

This code will populate the charts and `temperature` dashboard initially as well as when any change to the `temperature` or `humidity` keys take place.

Open up your dashboard again, and you should see the initial values of `temperature` and `humidity` getting populated on your dashboard. If you go to the Firebase console and manually change the values in the Realtime Database yourself, you should see them appear instantly on your dashboard without you having to do anything. Herein lies the power of connecting your application with the Realtime Database. We did not have to provision or manage sockets ourselves for any Realtime functionality, as it was provided to us out of the box by the Firebase platform.

Summary

This chapter started off with an introduction to the Firebase platform and the tools that it offers. It then went on to look at how our each tool that this platform provides would fit into our application's architecture.

After describing a new architecture to accommodate cloud-based APIs, we took a deep dive on migrating some of our code into it. This involved creating our first Firebase application, removing some of our older code, and introducing new code using the Firebase client side API to connect to the platform's cloud-based Realtime Database.

Overall, we completed the connection from client side to the cloud in this chapter. In the next chapter, we will be looking at how to link the other side of our application (sitting on the Raspberry Pi) to Firebase and thus enable our dashboard to show us actual sensor readings from our Pi, anywhere in the world, hosted on the Firebase platform.

12
Using Firebase APIs to Update Our Application

In the previous chapter, we were able to connect our frontend code to the Firebase platform's cloud APIs. We were able to retrieve and display mock readings that we got from Firebase and also updated them in real time with the changes that took place in the database. As a result, our entire API layer as well as our client-side static file has been moved to the cloud.

In this chapter, we will be dealing with the only part that we cannot move to the cloud: the sensor itself. This is the last piece in making our application completely cloud-based.

In this chapter, we will cover:

- The differences between implementing a server and a self-contained process
- Securing our application
- The application process architecture
- Implementation of the new architecture

Application server versus application process

As we move all our APIs to the cloud, we need to rethink what will now be going on the Pi. We still have to read data from sensors, and we still have to update an external data store. However, one thing that has changed is that our Pi is not serving anything anymore.

In the sans-Firebase implementation, our Pi used to act as the connecting block between our client-side scripts and our database. As a consequence of this, we had to run a server on the Pi that accepted requests and returned results:

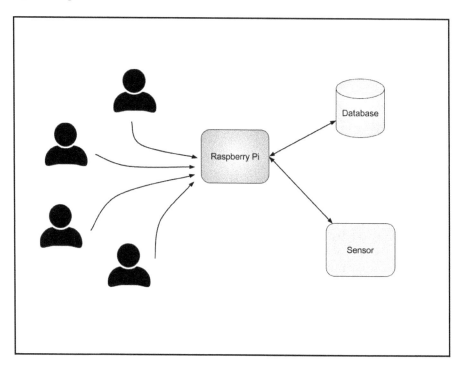

The most significant change now is that instead of being a listener, the Pi is going to be a notifier and update data on the Firebase Realtime Database. The middleware will now be the Firebase APIs:

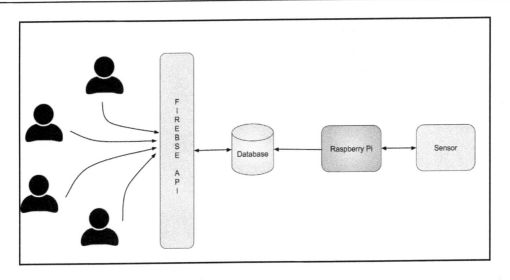

Securing our application

In the previous chapter, we were able to read from our Firebase Database to get our readings shown on the frontend. Now, the database has to be written to. Exposing our write functionality to the outside world the way we did for reading the data would have disastrous consequences, since we would essentially grant permission to everyone to modify our data at any time.

In order to make sure our data is modified only by us, we need to make secure modification requests. Before we get to the implementation, let's first create our credentials on Firebase; we will need these later when we have to access the database to update data.

In the Firebase console, go to the **SERVICE ACCOUNTS** section of your application settings, which can be found by clicking on the settings icon in the top right:

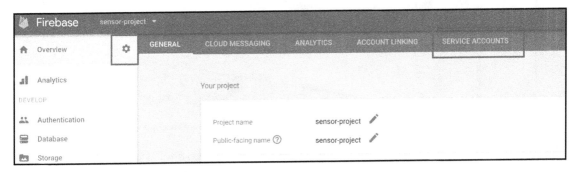

Under the **Firebase Admin SDK** tab, you can generate a new key for the **Node.js** SDK:

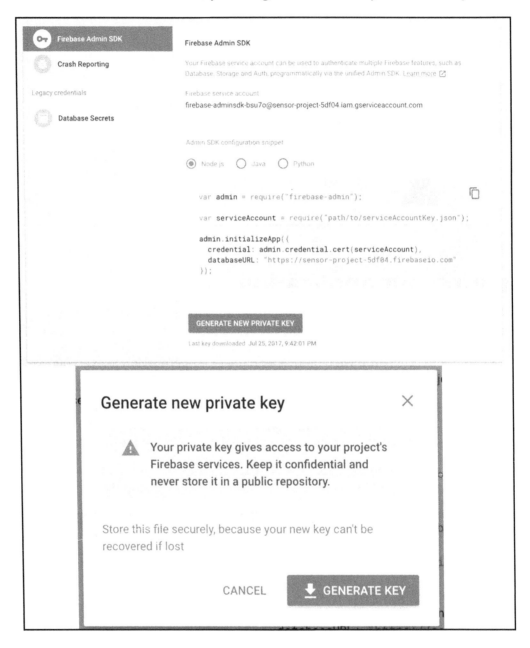

Once you have finished downloading the key, save it in a known location on the Pi.

Just like the advisory in the previous screenshot says, this key should not be shared, since it is basically what gives someone complete access to the Firebase tools for your application.

The application process architecture

Our application has many pieces--a lot of them new, and some borrowed from the previous implementations:

- **Firebase admin SDK**: This module is provided by Firebase, and acts as the interface between our server application and the Firebase cloud APIs. We are going to be modifying our data using this SDK, which will also make use of the key we downloaded in the previous section to authorize the API call.
- **Core module**: This is the core module of the application process, which will be responsible for initializing the Firebase SDK and updating the Realtime Database every time new readings come in. This will also be the starting point of the application.
- **Sensor module**: This module is borrowed from the previous implementations, and does not need to be changed. It will function the same way it was functioning before, with the purpose of obtaining readings from the sensor on our Pi's GPIO pins:

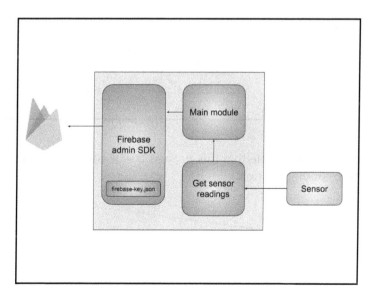

The overall flow will look something like this:

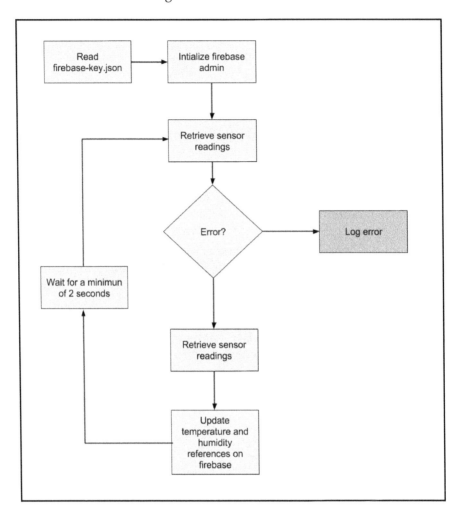

 It is important to note that this process is self-contained, and is closed to outside communication.

Implementing the application process

Since the application process is not a part of the deployed Firebase application that we built in the previous chapter, we will create a new folder for it (for this chapter, it will be named `firebase-process`).

First, we will be copying over the `get-sensor-readings.js` module from the previous implementations (shown here for reference):

```
var sensor = require('node-dht-sensor')

const getSensorReadings = (callback) => {
  sensor.read(11, 4, function (err, temperature,
humidity) {
    if (err) {
      return callback(err)
    }
    callback(null, temperature, humidity)
  })
}

module.exports = getSensorReadings
```

Next, we implement the core module:

```
/**
 * Import the "get-sensor-readings" module, as well as
 the firebase admin module
 */
const getSensorReadings = require('./get-sensor-
readings')
var admin = require('firebase-admin')

/**
 * Read the JSON key that was downloaded from firebase,    in this
case, it has
 * been placed in the "/home/pi" directory, and named     "firebase-
key.json"
 * You can change this to the location where your key is.
 *
 * Remember, this key should not be accessible by the     public, and
so should not
 * be kept inside the repository
 */
const serviceAccount = require('/home/pi/firebase-
key.json')
```

```
    /**
     * The firebase admin SDK is initialized with the key and      the
project URL
     * Change the "databaseURL" to match that of your      application.
     * Once the admin object is initialized, it will have      access to all
the
     * functionality that firebase provides, and can now      write to the
database
     */
    admin.initializeApp({
      credential: admin.credential.cert(serviceAccount),
      databaseURL: 'https://sensor-project-
    5df04.firebaseio.com'
    })

    /**
     * Initialize the database, and create refs for the      temperature
     * and humidity keys on our database. This is very      similar to the
refs we
     * created on the client side.
     */
    const db = admin.database()
    const temperatureRef = db.ref('temperature')
    const humidityRef = db.ref('humidity')

    /**
     * Create a task that runs after a fixed interval of time
     *
     * Here, we have set the interval to be slightly longer      than it was
     * before. This is to account for the delay that may      occur in the
network,
     * since we are not running the database on the local      machine
anymore.
     * If you find that the application is not communicating      with
firebase
     * as fast as you would like, try increasing this      interval based on
your
     * network speed.
     */
    setInterval(() => {
      /**
       * Retrieve sensor readings
       */
      getSensorReadings((err, temperature, humidity) => {
        if (err) {
          /**
           * If any error comes up, log it to the console and      return
from this
```

```
      * function call
      */
     return console.error(err)
   }

   /**
    * Finally, set the values for the temperature and     humidity
keys
    */
   temperatureRef.set(temperature)
   humidityRef.set(humidity)
  })
 }, 4000)
```

Start your application by running the following command:

`node firebase-process`

Now, navigate to your Realtime Database on the Firebase console, and you should see the readings updating every time a new reading is retrieved (the value that changes will show up in real time and be highlighted along with its respective key):

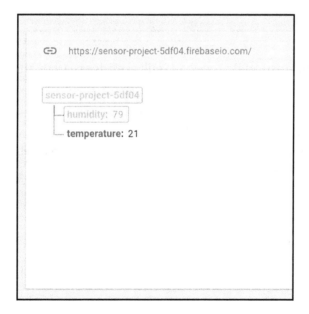

Now for the fun part: navigate to the location of the deployed Firebase application, and you should see the dashboard, just like it was before!

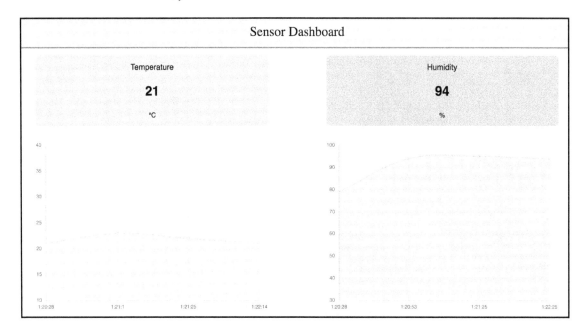

Moreover, some of the features that we had built ourselves earlier are already in place for us:

- The charts and display update instantly whenever a new reading is received, without any explicit HTTP calls.
- Only values that change are updated. If the sensor receives the same value twice, it does not send it over as an update.

Summary

We have finally built a cloud-enabled application that can be accessed by anyone in the world to view the readings that come from the sensor on your Pi device. The entire flow, from the sensor to the Pi, the cloud, the browser, and then to the user, is finally in place.

This chapter started by comparing the differences between the previous implementation that was running on the Pi and the one that we built here. This was a comparison between what compromises a server and a self-contained process. Next, the security considerations for write permissions was covered, along with some instructions on how to obtain these permissions through the use of the Firebase admin SDK. Then we discussed the detailed architecture of the application process along with a high-level overview of how it would work. Finally, we moved on to the implementation in our code by reusing some of the code from previous chapters and combining it with the Firebase admin tools to successfully push our sensors' data to the cloud.

Index

Write mode 57

X

www.ingramcontent.com/pod-product-compliance
Lightning Source LLC
Chambersburg PA
CBHW060556060326
40690CB00017B/3732